Cornwall & of Scilly

AA

M I N I G U I D E

FISTRAL BEACH, NEWQUAY

Author: Des Hannigan
Verifier: David Hancock
Managing Editor: Paul Mitchell
Art Editor: Alison Fenton
Editor: Sandy Draper
Cartography provided by the Mapping Services Department of AA Publishing
Internal colour reproduction: Sarah Montgomery

Produced by AA Publishing
© Automobile Association Developments Limited 2007

Published by AA Publishing (a trading name of Automobile Association Developments Limited,
whose registered office is Fanum House, Basing View, Basingstoke, Hampshire RG21 4EA;
registered number 1878835).

A03033F

TRADE ISBN-13: 978-0-7495-5583-2
SPECIAL ISBN-13: 978-0-7495-5690-7

A CIP catalogue record for this book is available from the British Library.

The contents of this book are believed correct at the time of printing. Nevertheless, the publishers
cannot be held responsible for any errors or omissions or for changes in the details given in this
book or for the consequences of any reliance on the information it provides. We have tried to ensure
accuracy in this book, but things do change and we would be grateful if readers would advise us of
any inaccuracies they may encounter. This does not affect your statutory rights.

Visit AA Publishing's website www.theAA.com/travel

Colour reproduction by Keene Group, Andover.
Printed in China by Everbest.

BEDRUTHAN STEPS

CONTENTS

Cornwall's long, dwindling peninsula reaches out into the Atlantic like a ragged claw and draws you westwards from the River Tamar to the towering granite cliffs at Land's End. Nowhere in that peninsula are you more than 20 miles (30km) from the county's superb coastline that runs through maritime healthland and coastal fields, along the edges of dramatic clifftops and past magnificent beaches and picturesque fishing villages turned tourist resorts. The rugged north is a land of mystery and legend and Atlantic-lashed cliffs, while the south is more passive, green and intimate, with deep bays and peaceful coves between bold promontories. Inland, you will find the old tin-mining districts, the lonely, granite heights of Bodmin Moor, the larger towns of rural Cornwall, and a maze of quiet lanes and tranquil villages to explore.

BUDE

Cornwall has more sandy beaches and coastline than almost anywhere else in Britain. Surfing reigns supreme in the north on a series of beaches between Bude and Newquay. This is where you'll also find superb family beaches with wide sweeps of golden sand.

In the towns and villages the distinctive character of Cornwall is just as potent. Walk around Launceston and discover how much of its rich history is still reflected in the façades of old houses and in the medieval pattern of its streets. At Falmouth, enjoy the seagoing atmosphere of one of the world's biggest natural anchorages. At Polruan and Fowey, experience a palpable sense of how the sea, and a remote coastline have shaped a colourful maritime past, when piracy and smuggling were a way of life.

With Bronze Age stone circles, cliff castles and a rich industrial heritage, Cornwall has a fascinating history. Geology and mining come to life at Geevor and Poldark mines with underground tours, while a stroll along the coastal path near Land's End and St Agnes reveals old engine houses peering out to sea from high cliff-tops. There is also Cornwall's spectacular Eden Project, the huge domes and the crowds, the restored Lost Gardens of Heligan, and more than 70 gardens scattered across the county, celebrating the kind climate.

The arts scene is as diverse as the scenery. Don't miss Tate St Ives and Penlee House Gallery in Penzance, and take in a magical open-air play at the Minack Theatre, a natural amphitheatre carved into the towering cliffs above Porthcurno.

Beyond Land's End, 30 miles (48km) offshore, are the Isles of Scilly, an immaculate archipelago that basks in the warmth of the Gulf Stream, with golden, crowd-free beaches, crystal-clear seas, quiet green corners inland, lush subtropical gardens and an altogether slower pace of life than you will find on the mainland.

Hartland Point

A39 Bideford

Bude

A39

Holsworthy

Tintagel Head

A30

NORTH CORNWALL

Launceston

A30

Tavistock

Trevose Head

Bodmin Moor

Padstow

Wadebridge

A388

SOUTHEAST CORNWALL

Bodmin

A39

Newquay

A30

A390

Liskeard

A38

Plymouth

St Agnes

St Austell

Fowey

Looe

MID-CORNWALL

A390

Truro

Rame Head

St Ives

A30

Redruth

A39

Dodman Point

LAND'S END PENINSULA

Falmouth

Zone Point

Penzance

A394

Helston

Land's End

A30

LIZARD PENINSULA

Gwennap Head

A3083

Lizard Point

ISLES OF SCILLY

11

HELFORD ESTUARY

ESSENTIAL SPOTS

Watch the surfers at Newquay...visit Cotehele, a beautiful Tudor house that lies amidst deep woods...don't miss the Eden Project, Cornwall's fabulous 'global garden'...drive the coast road between St Ives and St Just, one of the finest scenic routes in England...walk the cliff-tops at Land's End, the quieter reaches of the Helford Estuary or the lonely heights of Bodmin Moor...visit the fishing village of Mevagissey...explore Falmouth's maritime museum...cruise up the River Fal or take a fishing trip from Penzance.

1

1 The Lost Gardens of Heligan
The Giant's Head is a fun feature of these remarkable Victorian gardens, which were restored during the early 1990s after being abandoned for more than 80 years.

2 Tate St Ives
This wonderful purpose-built showcase for contemporary art, displays works by leading artists of the St Ives School.

3 Cotehele House
The well-preserved manor house and gardens of Cotehele lies in elegant seclusion and gives a fascinating insight into how wealthy people lived during Tudor times.

4

5

4 Eden Project

An orange tree flourishes in the Warm Temperate Biome, which emulates the natural landscapes and climates of the Mediterranean, South Africa and California.

5 Golitha Falls

The River Fowey flows through gorgeous oak and beech woodland in a steep-sided valley gorge, the Golitha Falls, on the southern edge of Bodmin Moor.

Day One in Cornwall

Cornwall and the Scilly Isles have so much to offer visitors – magnificent coastal walks, watersports, fine eating – it can be difficult to fit it all in, especially in a weekend break or a long weekend. These pages offer a loosely planned itinerary designed to ensure that you make the most of your time and see and enjoy the very best the area has to offer.

Friday Night

Stay in St Ives at The Garrack, a small hotel situated high above the town in secluded surroundings. Here you can enjoy views of the spectacular coastal scenery, including Porthmeor Beach, along with the welcoming atmosphere and wonderful food.

Wander around the harbour area at St Ives in the evening.

Saturday Morning

Stroll through attractive Fore Street, and on through charming narrow, cobbled streets of St Ives with their numerous galleries and craft workshops. Experience the essence of Cornwall portrayed through the great paintings at Tate St Ives and the Barbara Hepworth Gallery and Sculpture Garden.

St Ives' magnificent golden beaches are an alternative attraction when the weather is fine.

Leave St Ives on the B3306 north coast road, via Zennor and Gurnard's Head, through the glorious scenery of the Land's End Peninsula. Just before Morvah, at Trevowhan, turn left to visit the remains of a prehistoric burial chamber at Lanyon Quoit. Or remain on the B3306 and continue to Land's End to find spectacular views, exhibitions and wet weather attractions.

ST MICHAEL'S MOUNT

Saturday Lunch

Head for Marazion via the A30 and the A394, where a good place for lunch, in summer, is the Mount Haven Hotel at the eastern end of the town. There are splendid views out across Mount's Bay and to magical St Michael's Mount.

Saturday Afternoon

Reach St Michael's Mount, either on foot across the cobbled causeway or by ferry in summer if the tide is in. The Mount is cared for by the National Trust and both house and gardens are delightful. For children, the combination of castles and cannons in such a wonderful maritime setting is irresistible.

Take the A394 to Helston and through Gweek to Mawnan Smith. This is Cornwall's other landscape, a world of magical wooded creeks and quiet lanes, a delightful contrast to the rugged seascapes of St Ives and the isolated wild moorland of the Land's End Peninsula.

Saturday Night

Stay at the Budock Vean Hotel on the banks of the River Helford near Mawnan Smith. Set amidst beautiful gardens and parkland with a private foreshore to the Helford, the hotel includes a golf course among its leisure facilities.

Day Two in Cornwall

Your second and final day offers a choice of expeditions, on foot, through the Helford area, followed by a visit to one of Cornwall's loveliest gardens, Glendurgan. If the weather is bad, Falmouth, only a short distance away, has numerous wet-weather attractions.

Sunday Morning

If it is wet, drive north to Falmouth and visit the National Maritime Museum Cornwall, which transports visitors into the world of small boats and the port's rich maritime history, with entertaining interactive displays. The museum also has a Tidal Zone where you can take advantage of a natural underwater view of the harbour.

The best way to enjoy the beauties of the Helford area is on foot. The northern shore of the estuary, and its adjoining coastline, provides splendid walking.

Alternatively, a ferry trip from Helford Passage takes you to Helford village. From here you can enjoy an easy walk to Frenchman's Creek.

Helford can also be reached by a short drive round the end of the Helford. River. The route passes through Gweek where a visit to the Seal Sanctuary will delight children and adults alike.

FRENCHMAN'S CREEK

Sunday Lunch

For lunch, if you decide on a walk round the Mawnan Smith coast, then it might be best to take a picnic. If you cross to Helford, then try the 17th-century Shipwright Arms. This friendly pub, in a delightful riverside setting, provides a good selection of tasty meals.

Sunday Afternoon

Visit the National Trust's Glendurgan Garden, a valley garden of great beauty created in the 1820s. Children will love the laurel maze, which dates from 1833. The adjacent Trebah Garden, which lies in a steep-sided valley, is also delightful. This sub-tropical paradise is home to a large collection of rare and exotic plants. There are several paths through the garden that lead to a secluded beach on the Helford River.

Don't forget to make time for a delicious cream tea to round off your weekend tour.

Southeast Cornwall

INTRODUCTION

Southeast Cornwall is where singing rivers run south from Bodmin Moor through woods and well-farmed fields to reach one of the loveliest coastlines in England. It begins within sight of Plymouth at the peaceful Rame Peninsula, from where it runs west past spacious beaches to the port of Looe and the fishing village of Polperro. Further west the coastline traces its intricate way in and out of tiny coves and around handsome headlands as far as Fowey's graceful estuary and town. Between the granite country of the high moor and the coast are quiet villages and the bustling market towns.

POLPERRO HARBOUR

Unmissable attractions

Discover the secluded and wild Talland Bay, once the haunt of smugglers...
sit and watch the world go by at Cawsand...beach addicts can take their pick
of quiet beaches set in tiny coves on one the loveliest coastlines in Britain...
or those looking for more adventure can tackle walks and cycle rides on
East Bodmin Moor...visit the exquisite formal gardens, follies, mock temples
and Gothic ruins at Mount Edgecumbe Country Park...explore fascinating
towns and villages, such as Fowey and Looe...literary types can go in search
of Daphne Du Maurier at Menabilly, where the novelist made her home and
found inspiration for a number of her books.

1

1 Golitha Falls
The River Fowey enters a whitewater section of rapids as it makes its way through a steep, wooded valley gorge that is well-known beauty spot. The falls are best appreciated after a period of heavy rain.

2 Lanhydrock
In the care of the National Trust, Lanhydrock is part Jacobean and part Victorian structure. This imposing house, which gives a vivid picture of life in Victorian times, is set in magnificent grounds with colourful formal gardens. The higher garden, behind the house, is famed for its magnolias and rhododendrons bushes.

3 Talland Bay
Waves break on the bay's small sandy beach, which is flanked by flat beds of rock beneath the headland. It was used as a smuggling base during the 17th and early 18th centuries.

4

4 Hurlers Stone Circles

These three granite stone circles on Bodmin Moor date from the Bronze Age. According to local tradition they are men turned into stone.

5 Cawsand

Situated on the Rame Peninsula, the unspoilt fishing village of Cawsand is an ideal place to sit and relax away from the bustle and the crowds.

ANTONY HOUSE

Antony House, home of the Carew family for generations, is now cared for by the National Trust and stands in more than 100 acres (40ha) of woodland garden on the grassy banks of the Lynher River near Torpoint. The original Tudor house was pulled down in the early part of the 18th century and replaced by the finest Georgian house in Cornwall, perfectly proportioned with fine granite stonework facings of Pentewan stone and elegant colonnaded wings of red brick.

CALSTOCK

Calstock is Cornish, but its position is deceptive. It stands within a final enclave of Cornwall, set in lush countryside on the deep meanders of the River Tamar (the county boundary) that protrudes into Devon.

Calstock has been an important River Tamar quay since the Saxons arrived in Cornwall. For many centuries, sand and lime carried upriver on Tamar barges were used for improving the soil of surrounding farms. Tin and copper, and quarried granite from nearby Kit Hill, were transported back to Plymouth and at Calstock there was shipbuilding, and paper- and brick-making. Until the railway came to the Tamar

Visit

KIT HILL

The magnificent granite dome of Kit Hill rises to just over 1,000 feet (305m) above the town of Callington, about 4 miles (6.4km) northwest of Calstock. It stands in splendid isolation, as if torn between the granite masses of Bodmin Moor to the west and Dartmoor to the east. For centuries Kit Hill was quarried for stone and delved into for tin, copper, zinc, lead and even silver, but it is now a country park. The hill is crowned by an 80-foot (24m) chimney stack built in 1858 as part of the engine house of the Kithill Consols mine. There are pathways around the hill, including both a waymarked walking trail and a heritage trail.

Valley, full-masted schooners, steam-powered coasters, barges and paddle steamers all berthed at Calstock's quay.

Later, in the 20th century, market gardening in the surrounding area was a thriving business, but Calstock's great industrial days are long gone, leaving a rich heritage amidst the loveliness of the Tamar countryside. Calstock's great glory is its viaduct – built in 1906 with manufactured blocks, it is a triumph of good design and engineering. Today, the railway still links Calstock to the outer world, but it remains a river settlement and passenger boats from Plymouth still come upriver to tie up at Calstock, where pubs and restaurants, shops and galleries add to the attractions.

West of Calstock is Cotehele (National Trust), a Tudor house of great beauty that lies in deep woods in elegant seclusion. The Tudor style of the house has been preserved virtually intact thanks to the fact that in 1533 the owner, Richard Edgcumbe, built Mount Edgcumbe House on Plymouth Sound and made that the family seat. Cotehele then became a second home. Even the furnishings at Cotehele have a rare antiquity, with intricate tapestries of Flemish design and beautifully decorated furniture. There is no electric light at Cotehele, so avoid visiting the house on a dull day.

CAWSAND & KINGSAND

The villages of Cawsand and Kingsand lie on the picturesque Rame Peninsula within 3 miles (4.8km) of Plymouth; but because the high ground of Mount Edgcumbe lies between, there is no awareness of a large city and port being so close. The two villages, which now merge, were once divided by the old Devon–Cornwall border between Saxon England and the Celtic West – look for the sign on Garrett Street. The Saxons took control of both sides of the Tamar, a wise defence against the ever-present threat of Viking raiders.

For many generations those born in Kingsand were recorded as Devon-born, but today Cawsand and Kingsand sit comfortably together in Cornwall. Cawsand has a charming little square above its small beach and from here you can walk along the seemingly never-ending Garrett Street to Kingsand, through light and shade and past a grand clock tower. Explore the narrow alleyways and flights of steps that sidle to and fro above the rocky shoreline.

Running south from Cawsand is a level walk that leads along part of a Victorian drive, built by the Earl of Edgcumbe. Wealthy landowners of the 18th and 19th centuries often built such driveways through their properties in order to show them off to their full advantage to arriving guests. The way leads through shady woods to Penlee Point, where there is a delightful grotto built against the slope of the headland. From here you can enjoy exhilarating views of the graceful curve of Rame Head as it heads to the west.

Visit

MOUNT EDGCUMBE COUNTRY PARK

The original Tudor house at Mount Edgcumbe was destroyed by a bomb during World War II, a victim of the massive raids on Plymouth. It was rebuilt during the 1960s to replicate the original and has been handsomely restored. The landscaped park has many engaging features, such as follies, mock temples and Gothic ruins, and exquisite formal gardens. The park's woodland has a network of paths and fallow deer roam among the trees. Nearby is the little river port of Cremyll from where there is a passenger ferry to Plymouth.

EAST BODMIN MOOR

Cornwall's largest area of high moorland has been bisected by the A30, but the moor falls naturally into contrasting east and west sectors. The eastern side seems less wild and rugged than the undulating hills and rocky ridges of Brown Willy and Rough Tor to the west, while around

DOZMARY POOL

the remote village of Minions it has all the raw beauty of wild country. The moor has been torn apart in places. The ragged, gaping hole of Cheesewring Quarry above Minions is the result of a moorland industry that was as vigorous as the copper mining that left behind great engine houses nearby Phoenix United Mine. Cheesewring's granite was used to build Devonport Dockyard, Birkenhead Docks and part of Copenhagen Harbour and was included in the materials used in the Thames Embankment and Westminster and Tower bridges.

The quarry's name comes from the remarkable formation of layered granite that stands at its western edge, named after its similarity to a cider press used to squeeze the 'cheese' or juice from apples. It is formed by erosion of the weaker horizontal joints in the granite.

Close to the southwestern edge of the quarry is the reconstructed cave dwelling of Daniel Gumb, who was a stone-cutter in the

Visit

DOZMARY POOL
Atmospheric Dozmary Pool, on the A30, positively boils with myth and legend. The most enduring myth tells the tale of the infamous Jan Tregeagle, a rather nasty piece of work – actually a composite character of several generations of the Tregeagles, who were powerful lawyers, magistrates and land stewards between the 16th and 18th centuries, and notorious for their callous brutality and dishonesty. For their dirty deeds, Jan Tregeagle, a disgruntled spirit, is condemned by the devil to impossible tasks, such as baling out Dozmary Pool with a holed shell.

18th century. He built a much larger original cave dwelling here for himself and his family. Gumb was blessed with considerable intellectual gifts. He was known as 'the Mountain Philosopher' and was said to be well versed in astronomy and mathematics. Gumb's original cave was destroyed when

Cheesewring Quarry was extended in the 1870s, but the roof of the present one is part of the original and has on its surface a carving of one of Euclid's theorems. Minions Heritage Centre, in a Cornish engine house, has displays on the history of the landscape from the Stone Age, through 18th- and 19th-century mining and up until today.

Bodmin Moor is much older than its mining industry. Close to Minions village is a cluster of early Bronze Age (2500–1500 BC) monuments including the stone circles of the Hurlers and their adjacent standing stones. Craddock Moor to the west is peppered with burial mounds from the Bronze Age, hut circles of the Iron Age, and medieval field systems. North of Minions is Twelve Men's Moor and the rocky ridges of Kilmar Tor and Bearah Tor. Further north, a broad sweep of moorland runs through marshy ground to Fox Tor and then washes up against the asphalt boundary of the A30. To the west, the River Fowey flows from near Bolventor and Jamaica Inn, through a long, shallow valley. There are reservoirs with the characteristics of natural lakes at Colliford and Siblyback, and where the Fowey turns to the west at Draynes Bridge it pours through deep woods and moss-shrouded boulders at Golitha Falls. North of Minions, the moor drops suddenly into the deeply wooded valley of the River Lynher with peaceful hillside villages, such as North Hill.

FOWEY

Buildings crowd out Fowey's waterfront but there is a wonderful sense of unity within the jumble of narrow streets and there is access to the harbour and quay from various points. Fowey (pronounced 'Foy') was a major port from the earliest times. More than 700 seamen from the town and its surrounding parishes took part in the Siege of Calais in 1346 when the town supplied 47 vessels compared to London's 25. In return, Fowey was attacked and

FOWEY

Insight

FERRY EXCURSIONS

A relaxing way to visit Polruan from Fowey is to go by ferry. In summer a passenger ferry leaves from Whitehouse Slip, off the Esplanade (evenings from Town Quay); a winter service runs from Fowey's Town Quay. Take a bike on the ferry and follow the minor road east from Polruan to Lansallos and then on to Polperro, or walk along the coast path to Pencarrow Head and Lansallos. A summer passenger ferry also runs regularly to Mevagissey. Coastal and river cruises also operate from the Town Quay. A car ferry at Caffamill Pill goes to Bodinnick, across the River Fowey.

to equally lucrative, but honest, trade. China clay and the enterprise of the Treffry family brought prosperity, and today ocean-going ships pass upriver to Golant' quays from where clay is still exported.

Fowey draws you in from the long descent of Lostwithiel Street to Trafalgar Square, then on round the Town Quay and Webb Street. The buildings crowd in from all sides and even the dark-stoned Church of St Fimbarrus with its decorated tower seems to overhang. The true face of Fowey is seen from the river or from Polruan on the opposite shore. Tall houses rise sheer from the waterfront, and when night falls in summer the boat-bobbing river is starred with lights. From the bottom of Lostwithiel Street, the Esplanade leads southwest to Readymoney Cove, where a small sandy beach lies beneath tree-shrouded St Catherine's Point.

St Catherine's Castle crowns the Point; built between 1538 and 1542 as part of the chain of defences set

burnt by the French in 1380 and 1467. It was the Port of Cornwall in every sense and its seamen earned the title 'the Fowey Gallants'. These outstanding sailors were known for their arrogance and contempt for the law, and their energies soon turned to lucrative piracy. When Edward IV took a grip on the port, Fowey turned

up along the coast by Henry VIII in response to hostility from France and the Holy Roman Empire. The castle is reached by steep steps from the beach or by a leisurely track.

It is best to avoid driving through Fowey at the busiest times. The main car park at the entrance to the town is signed from the A3082. You will find a good mix of shops lining the bustling streets, along with fine galleries, craft and antique shops. Fowey's pubs are full of a sea-going atmosphere and there are several good restaurants. The museum is in the town hall at Trafalgar Square and the Tourist Information Centre is at the far end of Fore Street.

Overlooking the town is Place, the historic home of the Treffry family (now closed). The original house was built in the 15th century, more as a fortress than as a home, but Place was rebuilt in Regency Gothic style during the 19th century – 'Romantic baronial' may be a more apt description of this delightfully eccentric building.

Golant lies 1.5 miles (2.4km) north of Fowey from the B3269. In this charming village the Church of St Sampson commemorates one of Cornwall's great Celtic saints.

Insight

DU MAURIER COUNTRY

Cornwall's romantic image owes much to the novelist Daphne du Maurier, who, in 1926, made the Fowey area her home and inspiration. From 1943 she was a tenant of Menabilly near Gribbin Head and the house featured in *Rebecca* and *My Cousin Rachel*. The short story *The Birds* was set amidst the lonely fields of Menabilly Barton Farm, from where it took flight via Alfred Hitchcock's imagination to celluloid California. Du Maurier immortalised Jamaica Inn on Bodmin Moor and Frenchman's Creek on the Helford River, but she best revealed her profound love of Cornwall in her non-fiction book *Vanishing Cornwall*, a perceptive critique of the erosion of old values and landscape of her beloved Cornwall.

LUCY TOO
FOWEY

GRIBBIN HEAD

Southwest of Fowey, Gribbin Head (National Trust) shoulders out the western sea, preventing it from having too much influence on sheltered Fowey. The headland, always referred to as The Gribbin, is crowned with a bizarre monolith – the 84-ft (25m) Daymark tower painted in barber-shop red and white. The Daymark was erected in 1832 in order to distinguish The Gribbin from St Anthony's Head at the entrance to Falmouth Bay. The two headlands look similar from the seaward approach and sailors regularly mistook The Gribbin for St Anthony's Head, with catastrophic results when they sailed blindly into the shallows of St Austell Bay instead of the deep waters of Falmouth Bay.

Inland of The Gribbin is Menabilly, where Daphne du Maurier made her home and found inspiration for a number of her novels. In the eastern shelter of The Gribbin is Polridmouth Cove, a serene little haven with adjoining beaches and an ornamental lake.

The Gribbin can be reached on foot from a car park at Menabilly Barton, a mile (1.6km) inland. To the west, the tiny Polkerris faces into St Austell Bay. There is a car park halfway down the tree-shaded approach, from where it is just a short walk to the pleasant beach.

LANHYDROCK

The magnificent Lanhydrock House lies about 2.5 miles (4km) north of Lostwithiel via the B3268, or can be reached from Bodmin via the A30. It is approached along an avenue of stately beech trees, which leads through the beautiful parkland. On first sight the house gives every impression of being wholly Tudor. In fact, all that remains of the original house, built between 1630 and 1642 for wealthy Truro merchant Sir Richard Robartes, is the gatehouse, entrance porch and north wing. The east wing was removed, and the rest fell victim to a terrible fire in

47

1881, but, unusually for those times, the house was rebuilt to match the surviving part. The result is a powerful and dignified building.

The interiors are very grand, notably the Long Gallery, and there are lavish furnishings throughout the house. Of all the 50 rooms that are open, visitors tend to find the 'below stairs' sections of most interest, including the kitchen, larders, bakehouse, dairy, cellars and servants' quarters.

Lanhydrock is surrounded by beautiful grounds, with some pleasant rides and paths to stroll along. Adjoining the house are formal gardens with clipped yews and bronze urns, while the higher garden is famed for its magnolias and rhododendrons.

LISKEARD

With Bodmin Moor to the north, and Looe to the south, Liskeard is an ideal holiday centre. Liskeard was a Coinage town from medieval times and Coinage endowed the town with a status and prosperity that encouraged other business; copper mining during the 19th century further increased the town's wealth. When mining declined Liskeard continued to thrive as the focus of road and rail communications throughout east Cornwall and is still the northern terminus of the branch railway that connects with Looe.

Today Liskeard's attractive townscape reflects its prosperous history. The streets, quite narrow in places, are flanked by tall buildings. Fine individual examples include the notable Victorian Webb's Hotel, hip-roofed and stolid, which overlooks the Parade, whilst the Guildhall's Italianate tower dominates Market Street. In Well Lane, off Market Street, is the ancient Pipe Well; the water is now considered unfit to drink and the well is gated. Liskeard's Church of St Martin, the second largest church in Cornwall after St Petroc's at Bodmin, suffered some rather heavy-handed Victorian restoration and is a little dull.

Liskeard is a busy shopping centre, in keeping with its commercial traditions. On market days, the country brings a refreshing bustle to the streets.

LOOE

Looe is in two distinct parts that lie to either side of the merged East and West Looe rivers and are connected by a road bridge. It was a busy naval town during the 13th and 14th centuries and prospered until the 19th century importing lime and exporting copper. Tourism came early to Looe. It is said that the bathing machine came here as early as 1800 when war with France sent the leisured classes to southwest England in search of a home-grown alternative to French resorts. But it was the arrival of the railway, that led to the growth of the tourism that sustains Looe today.

The old town of East Looe is a delight. There is something of a French style in its ordered layout and in the way the tall buildings

Visit

THE LOOE VALLEY LINE

A trip on the Looe Valley Line from Liskeard to Looe is a stress-free way of going to the seaside and back, recapturing some of the excitement of those days when such a journey was a rare treat. The trains descend through the lovely East Looe Valley from Liskeard Station, with station halts on the way giving access along narrow lanes to pleasant Cornish villages such as St Keyne.

seem to accentuate the narrowness of the streets and passageways. The houses, some timber-framed but most of stone, are painted in a variety of colours. The old pilchard-curing cellars by the quay are built from unadorned stone and many of the cottages have the characteristic outside stone staircase indicating that the ground floors were used as pilchard processing cellars and net stores. There is an interesting museum of local history in the Old

49

POLPERRO HARBOUR

Guildhall in Higher Market Street. Looe is Cornwall's second largest fishing port and the fishing industry brings a pleasing bustle to the harbour and quayside at East Looe. Looe's viewpoint, Banjo Pier, can be reached from the quay and the very popular East Looe Bay beach.

West Looe was always the smaller settlement. It has a lovely outlook across the harbour to East Looe and the older parts of the town around Fore Street and Princes Square have some pleasant features. There is a big car park on the west side of the river at Millpool where there is a Discovery Centre.

The delightful Kilminorth Woods are reached easily from the Millpool car park. Waymarked walks lead through a splendid oak wood and alongside the West Looe River. The woods and river are rich in plant, insect and bird life. These include herons, which nest in the trees on the opposite bank. Further information can be obtained at the Discovery Centre.

LOSTWITHIEL

This attractive little town was a busy port throughout the medieval era until the silting of the river stopped vessels reaching its quays. Today the river is spanned by a 14th-century bridge with five pointed arches. Like Liskeard, Lostwithiel was a Coinage town, which prospered from the revenue earned from the lucrative administration of tin assaying and approval by royal seal. Near by are the substantial ruins of Restormel Castle (English Heritage), the best preserved military building in Cornwall. The castle was built during the Norman period on the site of a wooden fortification.

Modern Lostwithiel has lost much of its old townscape; the arches and buttresses of the Duchy Palace on Quay Street are all that are left of a much grander complex of buildings that included the Coinage Hall. One special glory is the 13th-century tower and 14th-century spire of the Church of St Bartholomew; the dramatic transition from square shape to octagon has a pleasing effect. There is a town museum in Fore Street. Coulson Park is by the River Fowey and there are riverside walks.

POLPERRO

The village rambles delightfully down to the sea. The pattern of narrow lanes and alleyways and steep flanking streets is set by the enclosing walls of the wooded valley within which Polperro lies is more engaging than in any other Cornish village. The inner harbour sits squarely among houses, and the boisterous stream, known as the Rafiel, pours into it beneath a Saxon bridge and beside the delightful House On The Props with its rough wooden supports. Polperro was always a fishing village, and remains so today, though its charm has made it one of the most visited places in Cornwall. Access to Polperro is on foot from a car park at Crumplehorn above the village. There are shops, art galleries, restaurants and pubs.

RAME HEAD

Rame Head is the dramatic western promontory of the Rame Peninsula; it has the well-preserved remains of a typical Iron Age fort. A medieval chapel and a hermitage once stood here and a small building survives, its roof mottled with moss and lichen, its walls rough with age. A warning beacon was once maintained on Rame Head as an aid to navigation, but tradition speaks of its more likely use by smugglers.

From Rame Head, the great crescent of Whitsand Bay curves to the west and the little fishing village of Portwrinkle. The beach is accessible only at low tide and ways down by steep steps and pathways are limited. Above Whitsand Bay, in a crook of the coast road, is Tregantle Fort, the most westerly of the line of defences that march from Fort Bovisand on the Devon shore of Plymouth Sound through a series of surviving bulwarks. They were built in the 1860s in response to fears of French invasion.

TOURIST INFORMATION CENTRES

Fowey
The Ticket Shop, Post Office,
4 Custom House Hill.
Tel: 01726 833616

Liskeard
Foresters Hall, Pike Street.
Tel: 01579 349148; www.liskeard.gov.uk

Looe
The Guildhall, Fore St, East Looe.
Tel: 01503 262072

Lostwithiel
Community Centre, Liddicoat Road.
Tel: 01208 872207

PLACES OF INTEREST

Antony House
Torpoint.
Tel: 01752 812191

Carnglaze Slate Caverns
St Neot.
Tel: 01579 320251; www.carnglaze.com

Cotehele
St Dominick, near Calstock.
Tel: 01579 351346

Fowey Aquarium
Town Quay.
Tel: 01726 816188

Fowey Museum
Town Hall, Trafalgar Square.

Mr Potter's Museum of Curiosity
Tel: 01566 86838

Daphne du Maurier's Smugglers at Jamaica Inn
Bolventor.
Tel: 01566 86025;
www.jamaicainn.co.uk

Lanreath Farm and Folk Museum
Tel: 01503 220321

Liskeard Museum
Foresters Hall, Pike Street.
Tel: 01579 346087

Looe Valley Line
Tel: 08457 484950

Lostwithiel Museum
Fore Street.

Lynher Valley Dairy
Upton Cross, near Liskeard.
Tel: 01579 362244;
www.lynhervalley.co.uk

Minions Heritage Centre
Tel: 01579 362350

Mount Edgcumbe House
Cremyll.
Tel: 01752 822236;
www.mountedgcumbe.gov.uk

Old Guildhall Museum
Higher Market Street, East Looe.
Tel: 01503 263709
Restormel Castle
Lostwithiel.
Tel: 01208 872687
Saltash Heritage Museum
17 Lower Fore Street.
Tel: 01752 848466;
www.saltashheritage.org.uk
South East Cornwall Discovery Centre
Millpool, West Looe.
Tel: 01503 262777
Tamar Valley Line
Gunnislake–Plymouth, via Calstock.
Tel: 08457 484950

FOR CHILDREN
Dobwalls Adventure Park
Dobwalls, near Liskeard.
Tel: 01579 320325; www.dobwalls.com
Land of Legend and Model Village
Polperro.
Tel: 01503 272378
The Monkey Sanctuary
Murrayton, Looe.
Tel: 01503 262532;
www.monkeysanctuary.org

Paul Corin's Magnificent Music Machines
St Keyne Station, between Liskeard and Looe.
Tel: 01579 343108
Porfell Animal Land and Wildlife Park
Lanreath, near Lostwithiel.
Tel: 01503 220211;
www.porfellanimalland.co.uk
Tamar Valley Donkey Park
St Ann's Chapel, Gunnislake.
Tel: 01822 834072

SHOPPING
Fowey
Antique shops, galleries and crafts, Fore Street area.
Liskeard
Open-air market with farm produce a speciality, Dean Street Cattle Market, Mon and Thu.
Trago Mills Shopping Centre
Two Waters Foot, on the A38, 4 miles (6.4km) west of Liskeard.
Lostwithiel
Antique shops in Fore Street.

55

LOCAL SPECIALITIES
CRAFT WORKSHOPS
Lanreath Farm & Folk Museum
Lanreath, near Lostwithiel.
Tel: 01503 220321
POTTERY
Fowey Pottery
10a Passage Street, Fowey.
Tel: 01726 833099;
www.foweypottery.co.uk
Millstream Pottery
19 North Street, Fowey.
Tel: 01726 832512
Louis Hudson Pottery Ltd
Unit 8-10, Moorswater Industrial
Estate, Liskeard.
Tel: 01579 342864
The Pottery Shop
Quay Road, Polperro.
Tel: 01503 272307

SPORTS & ACTIVITIES
ANGLING
Sea
Trips from Fowey, Looe and Polruan.
Shark-fishing from Looe.
Tel: 01503 264355;
www.looechandlery.co.uk

Fly
East and West Looe rivers. Permits
from Looe sub Post Office.
Tel: 01503 262110
Siblyback Water Park. Permits
available on site. Ranger.
Tel: 01579 342366
BEACHES
*Lifeguards, where indicated, are on
summer service. Dogs are not allowed on
several beaches from Easter Day to 1st
October. During winter, when dogs are
allowed, owners must use poop scoops.*
East Looe and Plaidy Beach
Popular beach.
Kingsand and Cawsand
Small safe beaches.
Looe Hannafore Beach
Shingle and some sand.
Millendreath Beach
near Looe. Close to Millendreath
Holiday Park.
Seaton Beach
Sand and pebble beach.
Whitsand Bay
Sandy beach but with limited and steep
access. Currents can make bathing
unsafe.

BOAT TRIPS

Calstock
Tamar River cruises. Plymouth Boat Cruises. Tel: 01752 822797

Fowey
River cruises, motor boat hire. Information from TIC.

Looe
Sea cruises from harbour.

Saltash
Canoe Tamar. Tel: 01579 351113

CYCLE HIRE

Bodmin
Glynn Valley Cycle Hire, Cardinham Woods, Margate. Tel: 01208 74244

Liskeard
Liskeard Cycles, Pig Meadow Lane. Tel: 01579 347696

Looe
Looe Mountain Bike Hire. Tel: 01503 263871

HORSE-RIDING

Liskeard
TM International School of Horsemanship, Henwood. Tel: 01579 362895; www.tminternational.co.uk

COUNTRY PARKS & WOODS

Cardinham Woods
Bodmin. Tel: 01208 72577

Kilminorth Woods
Discovery Centre, Millpool car park. Tel: 01503 262777

Kit Hill Country Park
Callington. Tel: 01579 370030

Mount Edgcumbe Country Park
Cremyll. Tel: 01752 822236; www.mountedgecumbe.gov.uk

CYCLING

South East Cornwall Discovery Centre
Tel: 01503 262777; www.cyclingcornwall.com

ANNUAL EVENTS & CUSTOMS

Fowey
Daphne du Maurier Festival, May. Fowey Regatta, Aug.

Liskeard
Carnival Week & Agricultural Show, Jun.

Looe
Carnival Week, Jul/Aug.

Polperro
Arts Festival, Jun.

The Plantation

The Coombes, Polperro, PL13 2RG
Tel: 01503 272223

A traditional Victorian tea room on the banks of the River Pol. Exposed beams and a fireplace create a cosy atmosphere. Friendly service delivers homemade cakes, excellent Cornish cream teas, and speciality leaf teas. You'll also find hearty lunchtime meals and a leafy terrace.

Muffins

32 Fore Street, Lostwithiel, PL22 0BN
Tel: 01208 872278

The Cornish cream teas are hard to beat at this light and spacious tea shop. Tuck into homemade scones, served with their Trewithen clotted cream and jam, all best enjoyed in summer in the lovely walled garden. Local produce features well in freshly prepared hot meals.

Edgcumbe Arms

Cotehele, St Dominick, PL12 6TA
Tel: 01579 351346
www.nationaltrust.org.uk

A National Trust tea room housed in a fine granite building beside the River Tamar on Cotehele Quay. Follow a visit to the medieval house and gardens, or a riverside walk, with soup, a ploughman's, or a cream tea.

Crumpets Tea Shop

1 Fore Street, Polruan, Fowey, PL23 1PQ
Tel: 01726 870806

Just a five-minute boat trip across the estuary from Fowey, Crumpets is a traditional tea shop decked out in yellow and blue, with sea-related prints on the walls. Just the ticket for light lunches, tempting home-baked cakes or a delicious Cornish cream tea, served with home-made jam.

TALLAND BAY

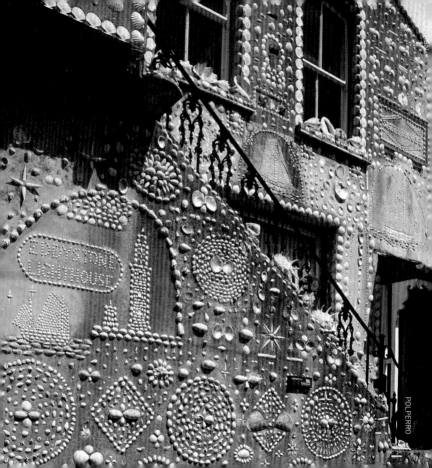

EDDYSTONE LIGHTHOUSE

POLPERRO

Crown Inn
Lanlivery, Bodmin, PL30 5BT
Tel: 01208 872707
www.wagtailinns.com
A fine 12th-century longhouse on the Saint's Way. The pretty garden overlooks the church. In winter, retreat into the low-beamed bars for a pint of Doom Bar beside a log fire. Changing menus include fresh Fowey fish, crab salad and steak and ale pie.

Halfway House Inn
Fore Street, Kingsand, PL10 1NA
Tel: 01752 822279
www.halfwayinn.biz
Wander down the narrow lanes towards the harbour and you will find this cosy inn among the colour-washed houses. Come for locally caught seafood in the dining room, perhaps roast garlic monkfish and smoked fish platter, and fish soup and ploughman's lunches in the simple, stone-walled bar.

Rashleigh Inn
Polkerris, Fowey, PL24 2TL
Tel: 01726 813991
Literally on the beach in a tiny isolated cove and known locally as the 'Inn on the Beach', Rashleigh Inn is worth seeking out for its magnificent setting. Order a pint of Cornish Knocker and head outside to the terrace where, in the evening, you can watch the sun sink into St Austell Bay. The food focuses on freshly caught local fish.

Webbs Inn & Restaurant
Pike Street, Liskeard, PL14 3HW
Tel: 01579 343839
www.webbsinn.co.uk
This rather classy bar and restaurant offers daily menus that feature the best local produce, perhaps pan-seared scallops with champagne butter and braised belly pork with apple and celeriac mash and bordelaise sauce. Lighter bites are served in the bar.

North Cornwall

INTRODUCTION

North Cornwall has superb stretches of coastline where a ten-minute walk can lead to the solitude of quiet coves and wooded valleys. Yet the region has accessible beaches where even on the busiest days there is room to spare. Padstow, Tintagel and Boscastle each have a uniquely contrasting appeal and, away from the coast, tree-dappled lanes link charming villages. On the ancient landscape of the high moorland, wind-sculpted granite rocks lie scattered across the lonely hills of Rough Tor and Brown Willy and, at Launceston and Bodmin, the spirit of an older Cornwall still lingers amidst the stonework.

TINTAGEL

HOT SPOTS

Unmissable attractions

Admire the dark shattered cliffs that rise for hundreds of feet from the rocky shores at Boscastle, the magnificent headlands of Trevose and Tintagel... head for the cheerful seaside towns of Bude and Padstow...explore the rock pools at Widemouth Bay...enjoy walking the quiet lanes that wander through mellow countryside between untouched villages and hamlets...go in search of the legendary King Arthur at Tintagel...enjoy an exhilarating coastal walk from Crackington Haven and admire the spectacular sea cliffs...relish the peace and quiet on West Bodmin Moor, where fantastical wind-sculpted slabs and pinnacles of silvery granite are scattered across the hills...take a steam train ride on the Bodmin and Wenford Railway.

2

1 Padstow

Still a busy fishing port of great character, Padstow's thriving fleet of fishing boats provide locally caught lobsters and crabs for restaurants throughout the country.

2 Widemouth Bay

The magnificent arc of Widemouth Bay draws families, who enjoy the wide expanse of beach and exposed rock pools at low tide, and surfers, who come to ride the high rolling waves of the Atlantic. The coastal path on the low cliffs backing the bay provides excellent views.

3 Tintagel

The natural splendour of North Cornwall's spectacular coastline as seen through the archway of Tintagel Castle, believed to be King Arthur's legendary Camelot.

4 Trevose Head

The Victorian lighthouse standing on the northwest extremity of the granite headland of Trevose Head, west of Padstow, was built to guide ships sailing into the Bristol Channel.

4

5 Port Isaac

The picturesque harbour at Port Isaac provides shelter for local fishing boats, and has fascinating rock pools exposed at low tide.

3

5

BODMIN

The small town of Bodmin lies on the southwestern fringe of Bodmin Moor, clinging to its own high hill, The Beacon. Bodmin was once the county town of Cornwall, but has long since relinquished that status to the grander city of Truro.

The town's development began in the 10th century after the monastery, which was founded by St Petroc at Padstow, was destroyed by Viking raiders. The monks withdrew inland for safety's sake and established their new religious foundation at Bodmin. They brought the holy remains of St Petroc with them and turned the town into the most important medieval religious site in Cornwall. Bodmin's name derives from 'menegh' meaning monks, and 'bos' meaning abode or dwelling. Augustinian monks later adopted the monastery, Franciscans founded a priory here, and the Shrine of St Petroc transformed Bodmin into an important and sacred place of pilgrimage.

Activity

BACK LANES BY BIKE

To the north of Bodmin, narrow winding lanes link the villages of Helland, Helland Bridge, Blisland, St Breward, St Tudy and St Mabyn. This is an area of peaceful mixed countryside and although divided by the B3266, the network of lanes connect across the main road at various points. The area can be reached from the Camel Trail, and offers some delightful cycling and testing navigation. There are steep inclines, but there is always the prospect of a pleasant inn and an occasional cream tea halt along the way. There are quiet churches too. A good circular tour from Bodmin links Helland Bridge, Blisland, St Breward, St Tudy and St Mabyn.

The Reformation and Henry VIII's Dissolution of Monasteries brought decline, although Bodmin retained its strategic importance for a time because of its position on the main route through Cornwall. Today, though the town has lost much of

71

Activity

STEAMING UP

The Bodmin and Wenford Railway operates steam trains along a delightful rural line from Bodmin to Bodmin Parkway Station, which is on the main Paddington to Penzance line. A branch line also goes west to Boscarne from where the Camel Trail can be joined. The restored Great Western Railway station in Bodmin is the headquarters and main station of the line. It is reached, from the centre of Bodmin, along St Nicholas Street, the B3268, and connections with main line services can be made at Bodmin Parkway. Passengers for the Bodmin and Wenford Railway are not allowed to park at the main line station.

its historic status, its robust Cornish character and strong community spirit remain intact. Bodmin is the ideal centre from which to explore north and southeast Cornwall.

Bodmin has some outstanding architecture, including a superb neoclassical court building dating from 1873 situated in Mount Folly. In Fore Street there are attractive stucco façades and the old cattle market has Doric piers and a frieze of rams' and bulls' heads. The fine Church of St Petroc is the largest in Cornwall and has some fine features. Bodmin Museum is in Mount Folly Square, on the site of the old Franciscan Priory, and The Duke of Cornwall's Light Infantry Museum is housed in the keep of the Victorian barracks. The Bodmin and Wenford Steam Railway Station is in St Nicholas Street.

BOSCASTLE

The sea can surge in and out of Boscastle harbour in a menacing way, entering between looming cliffs of slate and shale. The outer walls of the harbour are always damp with the sea and the salt air. Most of the area is owned by the National Trust, as are the adjoining clifflands of Willapark to the south and Penally to the north. The blow-hole in Penally Point, the headland on the northern side of the harbour entrance, is known as the Devil's Bellows and when the tidal and sea conditions are right, it throws a spectacular spout of spray right across the harbour entrance.

Boscastle was a busy commercial port throughout the 19th century – sea transport was usual throughout north Cornwall until the railway arrived in the 1890s. Up to 200 ships called at Boscastle in any one year, carrying coal and limestone from South Wales, wines and spirits, general goods and even timber from Bristol. Cargoes out of Boscastle included china clay and slate, and manganese from a mine in the Valency Valley above the village. Boscastle harbour was always difficult to enter and sailing vessels had to be towed through the entrance by eight-man rowing boats and by horses on towpaths. When big swells threatened to drive vessels against the walls of the channel, hawser ropes were made fast to the vessel from both shores, where teams of men braced the ropes round granite posts to hold the vessel in mid-channel.

Even on land there was no easy exit out of Boscastle and teams of horses hauled carts up and down the steep roads, which today carry traffic. The valley of the River Valency runs inland from Boscastle through deep woods, a peaceful contrast to the threatening sea.

Boscastle village proper is on the high ground and has some fine old buildings. There is a large car park near the harbour and, following the devastating floods in August 2004, the excellent visitor centre was granted a new harbourside location. On the north side of the harbour a National Trust information centre and shop is housed in an old blacksmith's forge. It is from here that you can get details of circular walks, a children's quiz and trail, and information on the local history, geology and wildlife of the area. In dull weather, Boscastle can have a certain eeriness, which may

BUDE

explain the presence of a Museum of Witchcraft by the harbour, full of enough wicca-related objects to send a chill down your spine.

On Forrabury Common, to the south of Boscastle, the National Trust has preserved the pattern of Iron Age land tenure, whereby long narrow strips of land were cultivated under a system called 'stitchmeal'. These Forrabury Stitches are still cultivated by tenants.

BOSSINEY

Bossiney, a short distance from busy Tintagel, is a quiet relief from too much Arthurian legend. Much of the coast at Bossiney is in the care of the National Trust. The beach below the cliffs at Bossiney Haven is reached by a steep path where donkeys once carried seaweed up from the beach to be used as fertiliser on neighbouring fields.

A short distance to the east lies Rocky Valley, where the river cuts through a final rock barrier into the sea. At the heart of the valley are the ruins of an old woollen mill. Within the ruins are small maze carvings on natural rock, most likely to be Victorian. Rocky Valley's river can be followed inland through the wooded St Nectan's Glen to St Nectan's Kieve, where a 60-foot (18m) waterfall plunges down a dark, mist-shrouded ravine. A fee is payable to view the falls and there is a tea garden above. The site can be reached by public footpath, which starts behind the Rocky Valley Centre at Trethevy on the B3263, a mile (1.6km) northeast of Bossiney.

BUDE

There are few more exhilarating beaches than Bude's Summerleaze when the sea rolls in long, unbroken waves. The Bude Canal shaped much of the immediate hinterland of Bude Harbour and is now a popular attraction for boating, walking and watching wildlife. The canal was built in the early 19th century to carry calcium-rich sand to inland farms, where it was used to enrich

Activity

STRATTON STROLL

Stratton was a prosperous market town for several centuries and its attractive, narrow streets reflect its ancient tradition. Therefore, a quiet stroll through Stratton is very rewarding. The town is reached by turning off onto the Holsworthy road from the A39, just east of Bude. There is a car park at Howells Bridge on the eastern edge of Stratton. From the car park, walk up Spicer's Lane to the church and from there into the centre of the town.

the soil. Bude Canal reached nearly to Launceston, but its full potential was never realised and its use declined by the middle of that century. The history of the canal is illustrated in the Bude-Stratton Museum at the Old Forge on the Lower Wharf.

Bude is a busy, friendly town – The Strand and Belle Vue are the main shopping streets. There is a good visitor centre in the car park near the harbour. A series of easily accessible and attractive beaches stretches north from Bude: Crooklets, Northcott Mouth and Sandy Mouth. The last two are almost covered at high tide. There are fine walks along the coast path to the north where the cliff-top area is level, cropped grassland. To the south of Bude, via a scenic road, is the vast expanse of Widemouth Bay.

Bude has few traditional buildings. The town evolved in the 19th century from a small fishing port through the grafting on of functional buildings, first for commerce, then for tourism. Just inland is Stratton. This medieval market town with a history that pre-dates Anglo-Saxon times was once the chief settlement of the area.

CRACKINGTON HAVEN

The mighty and dramatic bulwark of cliff at Crackington is best viewed from the southern approach. It seems to dwarf the cove and beach, its twisted and folded shale

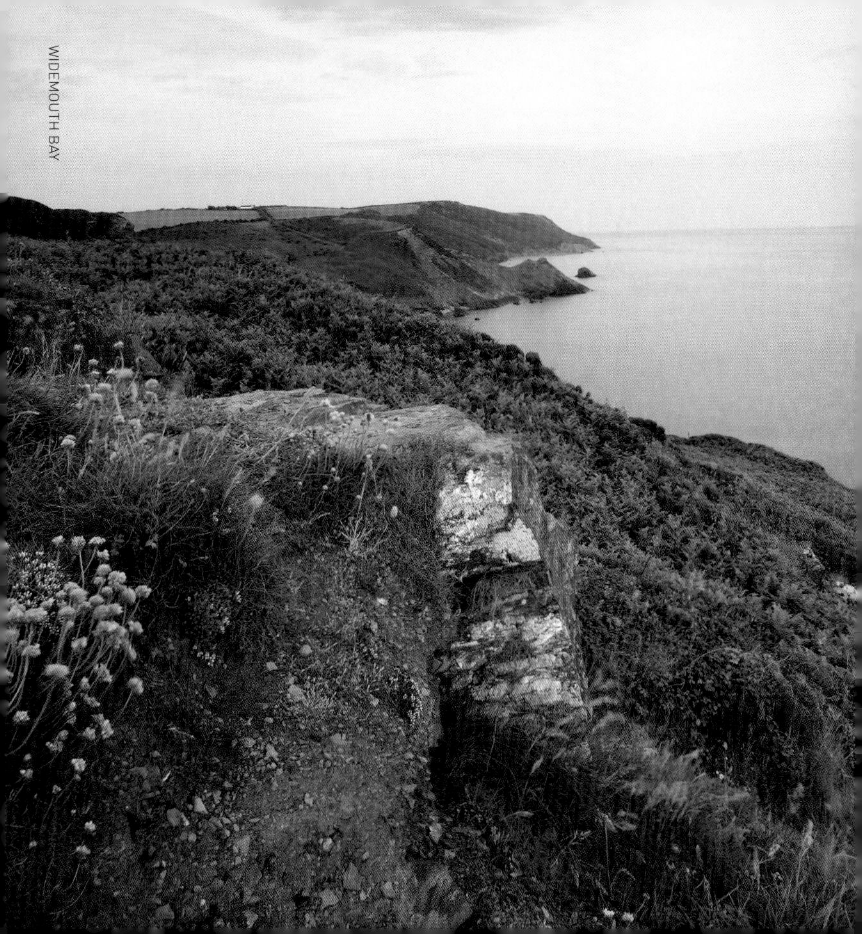

mellowed by swathes of grass and sedge. Crackington was a haven of sorts during the 19th century, but it was also a small port – small vessels simply ran on to the sand as the tide dropped to offload limestone and coal and to load slates.

The beach at Crackington is scant and stony, but the coastal walks to either side are magnificent. The coast path from Crackington Haven leads north to Castle Point. Take a deep breath for the climb out of the cove. There are the remnants of Iron Age embankments at Castle Point. A mile or so further on is Dizzard Point where an old oak wood clings to the slopes.

DELABOLE

Slate is believed to have been quarried at Delabole as early as medieval times. At 500 feet (152m) this is the deepest quarry in England; it is still being worked and its remarkable proportions can be seen from a public viewing platform. There is a showroom near

Activity

CRACKINGTON COAST WALKS

The stretch of coast around Crackington Haven can be reached less strenuously from the sturdy little Church of St Genny's, just north of Crackington Haven. The coast road south of Crackington is well supplied with parking spaces that give access to National Trust cliffland above Strangles Beach. This whole area of cliff has been altered by landslips, and though the coast path is safe and stable, do not stray from it. Just off the coast road is the National Trust farm at Trevigue. Below the farm is a wooded valley through which a fine walk leads down into Crackington Haven.

by. Delabole is a quarrying village with the sturdy character of similar communities in North Wales.

About a mile (1.6km) north of Delabole, along the B3314, is the first commercial wind farm to be established in Britain. The ten great white towers and their whirling vanes are quite sculptural,

Activity

OTTER SANCTUARY

The Tamar Otter Park and Wild Wood is situated in North Petherwin, which is reached by turning west off the B3254 at Langdon Cross, about 3 miles (4.8km) north of Launceston. Here, the Otter Trust's aim is to rehabilitate and breed otters for introduction to the wild. Dormice and several species of deer feature amongst other attractions.

generating electricity for 3,000 homes. Just south of Delabole is St Teath, a pretty village with an attractive church that has a refreshingly spacious interior.

LAUNCESTON

If Cornwall needs a metaphorical 'gateway', then Launceston, sitting astride the A30, qualifies, castle and all. But take care how you pronounce Launceston: say 'Lanson' – or else. Launceston was once a walled town, known as Dunheved, a powerful Norman stronghold, and the capital of Cornwall. The legacy of the town's long history is evident in its good architecture and the rather convoluted plan of its streets. To enjoy Launceston, park as soon as you can (there are car parks near the market and at Thomas Road and Tower Street) – Launceston's handsome South Gate forces traffic to pass through in single file while pedestrians pass comfortably three abreast beneath an adjacent arch.

At the centre of the town, the Square. has some very fine Georgian buildings, including the White Hart Hotel, which has the added flourish of a Norman arch over its doorway. The entrance to Launceston Castle (cared for by English Heritage) is reached by going down Western Road from the Square. It is impressive still, and though much has been lost, the typical motte-and-bailey structure survives. The stone keep and ruined gatehouse of the motte dominate the highest point of the complex.

The clay and rubble walls of the castle seem fragile enough now, but the overall impression is still one of strength and dominance. The Lawrence House Museum in Castle Street, housed in a mid-18th-century building (National Trust) showcases the town's history from the Bonze Age to World War II.

In contrast to friable clay, the Church of St Mary Magdalene at Launceston displays dark granite at its ornamental extreme. Every centimetre of this 16th-century building is covered with superbly intricate carving, described by Pevsner as 'barbarous profuseness'. The Launceston Steam Railway is based at the bottom end of St Thomas Road and runs for 2 miles (3.2km) through the valley of the Kensey River. There is an engineering exhibition at the station.

The village of Altarnun lies on the edge of Bodmin Moor about 7 miles (11.2km) west of Launceston. There is a car park just off the A30, from where it is a short walk

Insight

JOHN WESLEY AND METHODISM

During the 18th century the uncertainties of the mining and fishing industries resulted in periodic unemployment and hunger in local communities. The established Church was seen as the preserve of the gentry. Amidst these negative forces, the natural spirit of the Cornish people survived, but without direction. Violence, drunkenness, neglect and even riot were commonplace. Into this spiritual vacuum came John and Charles Wesley to preach passionately about redemption and non-conformity. Charles Wesley came first, but it was John who made Cornwall his special preserve, visiting about 40 times in 39 years.

to the village. The Church of St Nonna, known as the 'Cathedral of the Moor', has a noble tower and a spacious interior with some elegant features. These include a beautifully decorated Norman font and a large number of bench-ends with marvellous carvings. Cottages and other buildings in Altarnun are very fine. Neville Northey Burnard, the 19th-century sculptor, was born here, and his work can be seen in an early sculpture of the head of John Wesley, displayed above the door of the old Methodist chapel. He was also responsible for the Lander Memorial at the top of Truro's Lemon Street.

You will find that a fine contrast to Altarnun's 'Cathedral' is the Wesleyan Isbell Cottage at nearby Trewint. Here John Wesley and his fellow preachers stayed during their many visits to Cornwall in the 18th century. Digory Isbell, whose house it was, added a special 'prophet's chamber', has now been restored and is still very tranquil.

MORWENSTOW & COOMBE

The parish of Morwenstow lies at the very northern extreme of Cornwall in the narrow corridor of land that the infant Tamar River withholds from its Devon neighbour. Its coast is awesome, yet unexpected, when approached across the flat fields that end without much warning at the edge of 300-foot (91.5m) cliffs. This is the land of the famous Culm Measures, great twisted slabs of layered shale that rise from remote boulder beaches that are ribbed with fins of sea-washed rock.

Its natural beauty apart, Morwenstow owes much of its fame to the reputation of the Victorian parson, eccentric and unsuccessful poet, Robert Stephen Hawker, who was vicar at the Church of St Morwenna for many years. The church has good Norman features and is beautifully situated among trees in a shallow combe that leads towards the sea. The interior of the church has great repose and is pleasantly melancholic, especially at dusk, when there is a wonderful feeling of isolation. Visit Morwenstow with time to spare. The land around the church, and the stretch of cliffs to the west, are owned and conserved by the National Trust.

MORWENSTOW

Insight

MORWENSTOW'S VICAR

Morwenstow's Victorian vicar, Robert Stephen Hawker, was a marvellous eccentric, devoted to recovering the bodies of drowned sailors – who were in no short supply along this treacherous coast. But Reverend Hawker's stay at Morwenstow was fruitful in other ways. Rev. Hawker is credited with reintroducing Harvest Festival celebrations into the church, and wrote the *Song of the Western Men*, now Cornwall's anthem, especially at rugby matches. Hawker built a new vicarage – three of its chimneys were modelled on the towers of favourite churches; another on the tower of an Oxford college. The kitchen chimney was a model of his mother's tomb. While the chimneys smoked, Hawker is said to have smoked opium. He also dressed up as a mermaid on occasions. Say no more!

Southwards from Morwenstow is Coombe hamlet, set in a shady wooded valley that continues the theme of peace and tranquility. The river reaches the sea at Duckpool where the pebble beach has built up to dam a small pool of fresh water. Just north of Coombe, the coast path passes just above Lower Sharpnose Point, where spectacular natural piers of rock jut out into the sea like the massive walls of ruined temples.

Inland the smooth satellite dishes of the Cleave Camp Satellite Station strike an incongruous note amidst such raw natural beauty, and dominate the view for miles around.

PADSTOW

Padstow is a likeable, good-natured town in a fine position on the Camel Estuary. Its maritime history is a noble one, though it was often tragic. The shifting sand bar across the mouth of the estuary, the Doom Bar, is extremely dangerous at certain states of the tide and in heavy seas. Records show that over 300 vessels were wrecked here between 1760

PORT ISAAC

and 1920. At low tide, a vast expanse of sand sweeps away from Padstow, shading to gold towards the sea and to honey-coloured mud towards the inner estuary and Little Petherick Creek. Padstow's busy harbour has been modernised, but in keeping with traditional style. The buildings that cluster around it have great variety, and the maze of streets and narrow passageways behind it are pleasantly cool on sunny mornings. Padstow was a busy trading port from the earliest times, and Welsh and Irish saints of the Dark Ages landed here. St Petroc arrived from Wales in the 6th century and stayed for 30 years, founding a monastery, which thrived until AD 981 when it was destroyed by marauding Vikings. The present Church of St Petroc is pleasantly sombre within its shaded churchyard. The route of the old railway line, closed in 1967, is now the Camel Trail, a walking and cycle route. North of Padstow is Stepper Point, the fine headland at the entrance to the estuary.

The Saints' Way, *Forth an Syns* in Cornish, is a 28-mile (45km) route from Padstow to Fowey. It can be walked in two days and is best started at the Church of St Petroc. The first part of the route to Little Petherick, 2 miles (3.2km) south of Padstow, is worth doing for its own sake. Signposting throughout is generally good; a stylised Celtic cross motif is used on wooden posts.

TINTAGEL

Tintagel should not be missed. The focus of this relentlessly 'themed' village is the ruined castle moulded to the blunt summit of 'the Island' of Tintagel Head and approached across a narrow neck of land. The castle is 13th century, but the romance of the site has attracted competing claims for its origins: Iron Age enclosure, Celtic monastery, Roman signal station and, of course, the court of the King Arthur. The prominence of the Island suggests that it was used as a defensive site from the earliest times.

Barras Nose to the north and Glebe Cliff to the south are National Trust. It is tempting to say that the hinterland is in the care of the King Arthur industry, but Tintagel village offers much more than that. The wonderfully antiquated Old Post Office (National Trust) at the heart of the village is a delightful building. It is actually a small 14th-century manor house, with a central hall rising the full height of the building, and became a post office only in Victorian times. King Arthur's Great Halls in Fore Street is a remarkable token of dedication to a theme. The building was completed in the early 1930s and is devoted to Arthurian memorabilia and includes a fine collection of stained-glass windows.

WADEBRIDGE

The estuary of the River Camel narrows to a river's width at Wadebridge. The town was at the head of navigation of the Camel and was a busy port into the early part of the 20th century. The old bridge dates from the mid-15th century and it is said that it was built on foundations of woolpacks, the area being noted for its wool production. The bridge has been modified since but it still has a sturdy traditional style. To the west, modern technology has spanned the wider estuary with a lofty road bridge that has eased much of the town's traffic problem. The Camel Trail passes through the town along the track of the old railway.

WEST BODMIN MOOR

This area of Bodmin Moor lies west of the A30 and culminates in the wild and rugged hills of Rough Tor and Brown Willy, the latter is the highest point in Cornwall at 1,377 feet (419m). It is best approached on the A39 from Camelford, home of the North Cornwall Museum and Gallery; an art and craft gallery and Tourist Information Centre are in the same building, a converted coach house just off Camelford's main street. A picturesque riverside walk

TINTAGEL

starts from a passage through an archway in the centre of the town.

To the east, Bodmin Moor begins at the elegant rocky ridge of Rough Tor (pronounced 'Row Tor'), which, at 1,312 feet (400m) probably deserves to be called a mountain. Various paths across the wild, open moorland lead to a short climb to the summit which should not be too daunting for fitter walkers. The effort is rewarded with a spectacular all-round view. This is ancient landscape at its finest, littered with Bronze-Age hut circles and other remains. To the north Showery Tor has fantastic wind-sculpted summit rocks; to the east is Brown Willy whose proper name derives from 'bron' for hill and 'ewhella' for highest. Brown Willy is less dragon-backed than Rough Tor, but more remote.

Amid all this lies the valley of the De Lank River draining southwards past the secretive Garrow Tor and Hawk's Tor. Most of the moorland is privately owned grazing common. Dogs should not be let off the leash.

Activity

THE CAMEL TRAIL

The route of the old Atlantic Coast Express, from Wadebridge to Padstow, is now the main part of the Camel Trail, a recreational walking, horse-riding and cycling route which passes through varied countryside alongside the River Camel. This traffic-free trail is ideal for all the family as the surface is mainly smooth and virtually level with one gentle climb from Wadebridge to Poley's Bridge. It is ideal for wheelchair users, prams and buggies and those who have difficulty walking on uneven surfaces. There are plenty of benches and picnic tables along the way where you can stop and enjoy the views. The Camel Trail can be joined at several points: Padstow, Wadebridge and at Boscarne Junction to the west of Bodmin, where it swings north to continue through Hellandbridge to terminate at Poley's Bridge. The full extent of the Camel Trail is 18 miles (29km).

TOURIST INFORMATION CENTRES

Bodmin
Shire Hall, Mount Folly.
Tel: 01208 76616;
www.bodminlive.com

Bude
The Crescent Car Park.
Tel: 01288 354240; www.visitbude.info

Camelford
North Cornwall Museum, The Clease.
Tel: 01840 212954

Launceston
Market Place.
Tel: 01566 772321;
www.visitlaunceston.co.uk

Padstow
North Quay.
Tel: 01841 533449

Wadebridge
Rotunda Building, Eddystone Road.
Tel: 01208 813725;
www.visitwadebridge.com

PLACES OF INTEREST

Arthurian Centre
Slaughterbridge, Camelford.
Tel: 01840 212450;
www.arthur-online.com

Bodmin & Wenford Railway
General Station. Tel: 01208 73666;
www.bodminandwenfordrailway.co.uk

Bodmin Jail
Berrycoombe Road. Tel: 01208 76292

Bodmin Museum
Mount Folly Square. Tel: 01208 77067

Bude-Stratton Museum
Lower Wharf, Bude.
Tel: 01288 353576

Delabole Slate Quarry
Pengelly Road, Delabole.
Tel: 01840 212242;
www.delaboleslate.co.uk

Duke of Cornwall's Light Infantry Museum
The Keep, Bodmin.
Tel: 01208 72810

John Betjeman Centre
Southern Way, Wadebridge.
Tel: 01208 812392

King Arthur's Great Halls
Fore Street, Tintagel.
Tel: 01840 770526;
www.kingarthursgreathall.com

Launceston Castle
Tel: 01566 772365

Launceston Steam Railway
St Thomas Road, Launceston
Tel: 01566 775665

Lawrence House Museum
9 Castle Street, Launceston.
Tel: 01566 773277

Long Cross Victorian Gardens
St Endellion, near Port Isaac.
Tel: 01208 880243;
www.longcrosshotel.co.uk

The Museum of Witchcraft
The Witches House, Boscastle Harbour.
Tel: 01840 250111

National Lobster Hatchery
South Quay, Padstow.
Tel: 01841 533877

North Cornwall Museum and Gallery
The Clease, Camelford.
Tel: 01840 212954

Pencarrow House and Gardens
Washaway, near Bodmin.
Tel: 01208 841369;
www.pencarrow.co.uk

Prideaux Place
Padstow.
Tel: 01841 532411/2;
www.prideauxplace.co.uk

The Tamar Otter Park
North Petherwin, near Launceston.
Tel: 01566 785646

Tintagel Castle
Tel: 01840 770328

FOR CHILDREN

Colliford Lake Park
Bolventor, Bodmin Moor.
Tel: 01208 821469

Cornwall's Crealy Great Adventure Park
Tredinnick, Wadebridge.
Tel: 01841 541215; www.crealy.co.uk

SHOPPING

Bodmin
Street market, Mount Folly,
Sat morning.

Padstow
Market, Tue, May–Sep.

LOCAL SPECIALITIES

Crafts
Lower Wharf Gallery, by Bude Canal.

Pottery
Boscastle Pottery, The Old Bakery
Tel: 01840 250291

SPORTS & ACTIVITIES

ANGLING

Sea
Various trips from Padstow harbour; enquire locally.

Coarse
Tamar Lakes Water Park, near Bude. Permit required. Tel: 01409 211514
Crowdy Reservoir, near Camelford
Tel: 01409 211514

BEACHES
Lifeguards, where indicated, are on summer service. Dogs are not allowed on several beaches from Easter Day to 1st October. During winter, when dogs are allowed, owners must use poop scoops.

Bude
Crooklets Beach: good surfing. Lifeguard.

Constantine Bay
Good sandy area. Limited parking. Lifeguard.

Crackington Haven
Pebbly beach with sand at low tide. Lifeguard.

Daymer Bay
Sheltered sandy beach with dunes. Currents can be dangerous.

Harlyn Bay
Sheltered sandy beach with dunes. Lifeguard.

Padstow
Fine beaches but beware of dangerous tidal currents.

Polzeath, Hayle Bay
Busy family beach. Lifeguard.

Trebarwith Strand
South of Tintagel. Sand and rocks. Lifeguard.

Trevone Bay
Pleasant sandy cove. Lifeguard.

Treyarnon Bay
Good family beach. Lifeguard.

Widemouth
Good for families and surfing. Lifeguard where indicated.

BOAT TRIPS

Bude
Rowing boats and canoes for hire at Bude Canal.

Padstow
Pleasure trips available from the harbour.

CYCLING
www.cyclingcornwall.com

The Camel Trail
Tel: 01208 815631
CYCLE HIRE
Bodmin
Bodmin Cycle Hire, Bodmin and
Wenford Railway station.
Tel: 01208 73555
Bude
North Coast Cycles, 2 Summerleaze
Avenue. Tel: 01288 352974
Padstow
Padstow Cycle Hire Ltd, South Quay.
Tel: 01841 533533;
www.padstowcyclehire.com
Wadebridge
Bridge Bike Hire, Eddystone Road.
Tel: 01208 813050;
www.bridgebikehire.co.uk
Camel Trail Cycle Hire, Trevanson
Street. Tel: 01208 814104
Cycle Revolution, Eddystone Road.
Tel: 01208 812021
HORSE-RIDING
Boscastle
Tredole Trekking, Trevalga.
Tel: 01840 250495

Bude
Maer Stables, Crooklets.
Tel: 01288 354141
Launceston
Elm Park Equestrian Centre, North
Beer, Boyton.
Tel: 01566 785353
WATERSPORTS
Bude
Outdoor Adventure, Widemouth Bay.
Tel: 01288 362966;
www.outdooradventure.co.uk
Polzeath
Surfs Up, Polzeath.
Tel: 01208 862003;
www.surfsupsurfschool.com

ANNUAL EVENTS & CUSTOMS
Bodmin
Riding and Heritage Day, Jul.
Bude
Jazz Festival, end of Aug.
Padstow
May Day Festival.
Wadebridge
Royal Cornwall Show, Jun.

TEA ROOMS

Rectory Farm Tea Rooms
Morwenstow, Bude, EX23 9SR
Tel: 01288 331251
Dating back to 1296, this working farmhouse offers good honest cooking. Enjoy the peaceful garden on summer days or take refuge in the cosy rooms with big open fireplaces on cold days. Freshly prepared food includes ploughman's platters, soups and pasties, and light, home-baked scones served warm with clotted cream.

The Tea Shop
6 Polmorla Road, Wadebridge, PL27 7ND
Tel: 01208 813331
Fresh local produce takes pride of place on the menu at this bright and cosy tea shop, and everything is prepared on the premises. Expect to choose from a range of 40 teas and around 30 cakes, including boiled fruit cake and apple and almond cake. Light lunches are also available.

Rick Stein's Café
10 Middle Street, Padstow, PL28 8AP
Tel: 01841 532700
www.rickstein.com
The most relaxed of Rick Stein's restaurants is a casual café-with-rooms decked out with a nautical theme. It's open all day, so call in for breakfast or an excellent cappuccino and peruse the papers, or arrive early for deliciously simple lunches and dinners – salt-and-pepper prawn, whole grilled mackerel with tomato and onion salad, or chickpea, parsley and salt cod stew.

PORT ISAAC

Mill House Inn

Trebarwith, Tintagel, PL34 0HD
Tel: 01840 770200
www.themillhouseinn.co.uk
A converted 18th-century mill house halfway up the wooded valley from the beach at Trebarwith. The bar is big, with flagged floors, a wood-burning stove, and Sharp's ales on tap. The dining room has a relaxed, bistro feel Dishes include brill pan-fried with king prawns and mussels with a chilli and coriander dressing.

Bush Inn

Morwenstow, Bude, EX23 9SR
Tel: 01288 331242
www.bushin-morwenstow.co.uk
The historic Bush Inn is set in an isolated cliff-top hamlet. Flagstones, beams, inglenooks and old settles preserve the character of the bar. There's a contemporary feel to the dining room which offers dishes such as, Thai scallop salad and whole roast John Dory, while traditional ploughman's and cream teas are served in the bar.

Old Inn

Church Town, St Breward,
Bodmin Moor, PL30 4PP
Tel: 01208 850711
www.theoldinnandrestaurant.co.uk
This low, whitewashed moorland inn has a bar that dates back to the 11th century. The bar sports thick beams, oak settles, slate floors and roaring log fires. The food is wholesome, unpretentious and not for the faint-hearted – portions are very generous.

Bay View Inn

Widemouth Bay, Bude, EX23 0AW
Tel: 01288 361273
www.bayviewinn.co.uk
Savour a pint of Sharp's on the sun deck, absorb the view across the glorious sandy beach – just two reasons to visit this superbly located free house on Cornwall's north coast. Add a lively, candlelit bar, imaginative, freshly prepared food using locally sourced produce, and very stylish bedrooms, if you choose to stay here.

NEWQUAY

Mid-Cornwall

INTRODUCTION

The contrast between the north and south coasts of mid-Cornwall is quite dramatic. The north coast – famous for surfing beaches, such as Newquay – is also home to delightful family beaches backed by sand dunes and flanked by magnificent headlands. The south is more placid, its beaches quieter and pleasantly remote, while around Mevagissey and the exquisite Roseland Peninsula, there is a lush quality to the landscape. In the east is St Austell and Cornwall's famous white 'Alps' of the clay country, home of the Eden Project, and, at its heart, the busy cathedral city of Truro.

BEDRUITHAN STEPS

Unmissable attractions

Explore St Agnes, a friendly unassuming coastal village surrounded by some intriguing tin-mining remains...discover the old mining towns of Camborne and Redruth, rich in industrial archaeology and home of Cornwall's School of Mines...walk along Perranporth, one of Cornwall's vast beaches, where acres of wave-rippled sand are exposed at low tide...catch the surf (or watch others) at Newquay, Britain's premier surfing venue where the magic mix of Atlantic swell and golden sand draws surfers from all over the world...enjoy quiet woodland trails and admire the acid-loving camellias, magnolias and rhododendrons at Trelissick...be captivated by the charms of Mevagissey... shop in the busy city of Truro and spend time exploring its fine cathedral.

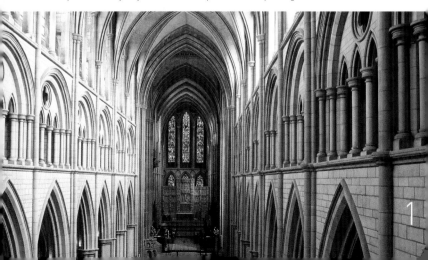

1 Truro Cathedral

Standing in the heart of the city, the cathedral was built of local granite and Bath stone in the 19th century. Inside, soaring arches and slender pillars, bathed in a golden light, lead the eye up to to the vaulted roof.

2 The Eden Project

Alongside all the magnificent plants throughout the Eden Project you will find exciting and informational multimedia and sculptural exhibits depicting the exotic world of plants, their products and habitats.

2

3 Watergate Bay
Surfers come to Watergate Bay, just north of Newquay, to enjoy some of the best waves that Cornwall has to offer.

4 The Lost Gardens of Heligan
Shady tree ferns, palms and bamboo are among a few of the exotic trees and shrubs that flourish in the jungle section of the lush green gardens of Heligan.

3

4

5 Mevagissey
The charm of Mevagissey's narrow streets, old houses and picturesque harbour dotted with fishing boats attracts many visitors.

5

BEDRUTHAN STEPS

BEDRUTHAN STEPS

The flat, unremarkable countryside that lies inland from Bedruthan Steps belies the stupendous nature of the area's coastline. Access to the beach at Bedruthan has been difficult over the years because of the crumbling nature of the cliffs, but the National Trust has built a secure stairway from the clifftop at Carnewas. The famous 'Steps' are the weathered rock stacks that stand in bold isolation amidst the sand. Bedruthan Steps are the result of sea erosion on the caves and arches in the friable slate cliffs. They have colourful local names, such as Queen Bess, Samaritan Island and Diggory's Island. According to local legend, a mythical giant, Bedruthan, was reputed to use the stacks as stepping stones; but to nowhere in particular it seems. There is a National Trust shop and café on the clifftop in what was the office building of the old Carnewas iron mine. It is a delightful spot to indulge in a cream tea.

CAMBORNE

Camborne is not picturesque and the locals would not thank you for saying otherwise. The town has borne the brunt of Cornish industrialisation and of the strip development that the linear shape of the county dictated, but the town thrives still, in spite of the current cessation of work at the nearby South Crofty tin mine. There are gems of industrial archaeology at Pool, midway between Camborne and Redruth, where the National Trust has restored two great steam engines. They were used for pumping water from a depth of 1,640 feet (500m) and for winding men and ore up and down the mine shafts. Near by is the Industrial Discovery Centre, which provides an overview of Cornwall's industrial heritage and incorporates a fascinating audio-visual presentation.

Camborne was associated with the greatest of Cornish inventors, Richard Trevithick (1771–1833), whose statue stands outside Camborne Public Library

Insight

THE CORNISH MINER ABROAD

There is a saying that says at the bottom of a deep mine anywhere in the world, you will find a Cornish miner digging even deeper. There is some truth in this. It was the thousands of miners forced into emigration by mining slumps at home that made the Cornish so famous abroad. A particularly severe slump in copper mining during the 1860s caused many miners to emigrate to the Americas, South Africa and Australia. 'Cousin Jacks', as they were known, either sent money home or brought their families to join them, and Cornish names and traditions still survive in far-flung places.

in Trevenson Street. Trevithick was born at nearby Illogan. He married a daughter of the Hayle foundry family, the Harveys, and devoted his life to industrial invention and development. Trevithick designed steam engines and invented a steam threshing machine, an early road vehicle, and the first railway engine. Camborne celebrates its famous son with a special Trevithick Day in April. A small museum in the library has displays on mining and archaeology and on Trevithick's work.

Near by, Tehidy Country Park has shady leafy walks, streams and ornamental lakes, and is close to the invigorating north coast.

CHARLESTOWN

Charlestown is St Austell's gateway to the sea. The creation of the port in the late 18th century was the brainchild of local entrepreneur Charles Rashleigh and became known as 'Charles's town'.

The harbour was originally called West Polmear, a modest fishing cove where ships ran on to the beach to load copper ore and china clay from the developing industries of the St Austell area. Rashleigh also commissioned Eddystone Lighthouse engineer John Smeaton to build a deep harbour with lock gates.

EDEN PROJECT

The road to Charlestown is a fine, broad avenue in keeping with the breadth of Rashleigh's ambitions for the town. Square-rigged ships are now berthed in the harbour and can be visited during the summer. There is a Shipwreck, Rescue and Heritage Centre and nautical pubs.

Charlestown is a great favourite with film makers, and its harbour and sailing ships were used in the 1970s television series *The Onedin Line* and and 1976 film *The Eagle Has Landed*.

CRANTOCK

Crantock stands beside the long, narrow estuary of the River Gannel. At the heart of the village is the serene little Round Garden, now in the care of the National Trust. Crantock also has two holy wells, one in the centre, the other on the road to the beach. The Church of St Carantocus has 13th- and 14th-century features. There are shops and pubs in the village, and a tea garden that is open during the summer. Crantock beach is just west of the village; above the beach is Rushy Green, an area of sand dunes. To the west of Crantock is West Pentire, where there is a car park. From here you can take the zigzag track south to Porth Joke, also known as Polly Joke, a charming sand-filled cove.

Holywell Bay, further south again, is reached from Crantock by following an unclassified road south to Cubert, from where a right turn leads to the car park above Holywell's sandy beach.

THE EDEN PROJECT

Cornwall's spectacular 'global garden', the Eden Project, has transformed a one-time clay-quarrying pit at Bodelva near St Austell into one of Europe's most popular tourist attractions. Eden is housed within futuristic glass biomes – enormous domed conservatories within which the main climate systems of the world have been recreated.

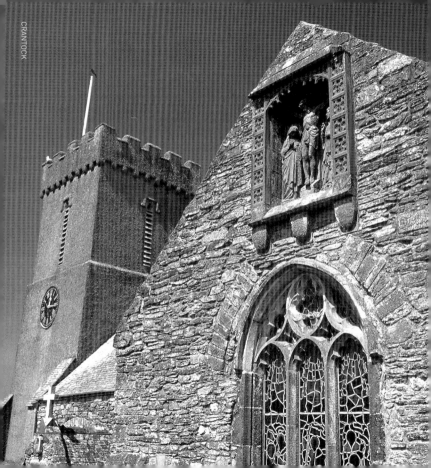
CRANTOCK

GODREVY HEAD

The National Trust property of Godrevy Head stands at the eastern end of St Ives Bay and is the first of a sequence of high rugged cliffs of dark slate that run uninterruptedly to the northeast. Offshore from the headland stands Godrevy Island and its crowning lighthouse. There is ample parking at Godrevy Head on grassy downs that are reached along a winding road. Paths lead across and around the headland; the offshore waters attract inquisitive grey seals. To the south lies Gwithian beach, and inland is the village of Gwithian where there is a handsome church and an attractive pub.

Inside the huge Humid Tropics Biome pathways wind through the plants of West Africa, Amazonia, Malaysia and Oceania. There are even teak, mahogany and rubber trees, interspersed with bamboo, and a host of tropical plants, all fed by the moisture from a waterfall.

The smaller Warm Temperate Biome replicates the habitats of Southern Africa, the Mediterranean and California, with hundreds of vividly coloured flowers intermingled with olive groves and vines. From the main biomes you move into the 'Outdoor' Biome', covering 30 acres (12ha), where local plants flourish alongside those of the Himalayas, Chile and Australasia.

GORRAN HAVEN & THE DODMAN

Gorran Haven lies just south of Mevagissey at the seaward end of a shallow valley. Steep lanes and passageways climb from the harbour and an intriguing little chapel built on solid rock dates from the 15th century. South of Gorran Haven, the mighty Dodman Point thrusts its bull's head into the seaway. The Dodman, as it is commonly known, is 373 feet (114m) high. The Iron Age earthworks that enclose the seaward area of the Dodman are over 2,000 feet (609m) long and 20 feet (6m) high.

MEVAGISSEY

The picturesque little village of Mevagissey tucks neatly into the land and guards itself within the folded arms of its inner and outer harbours. It is one of Cornwall's most popular resorts, a fishing village whose simple charm attracts tourists in their thousands. It became a leading pilchard fishing port in Tudor times and continued as such into the 21st century. For many years it supplied the navy with pilchards, which became known as Mevagissey Ducks.

Today there is still a fishing fleet here but one that is more diverse. Like most Cornish fishing villages Mevagissey has great character, especially in the old part of the village that lies between the Fountain Inn and the Battery on the eastern side of the harbour. Many of the houses are pleasingly colour-washed and despite the fact that the harbour area has seen some modern development, the village has retained its Cornish charm.

The inner harbour is a place to linger on warm summer days – seats line the quays but competition is fierce. The narrow alleys and streets of the village draw you on to the next corner, past galleries and gift shops and in and out of light and shade. The refurbished aquarium at the old lifeboat house on the South Quay gives an insight into life in deeper waters (the profits go to the upkeep and improvement of Mevagissey harbour). There is a fine little museum of local history on the East Quay and, engagingly for this sea-going town, there is a model railway museum in Meadow Street.

Heligan was once a lost garden, but now is one of the most popular tourist attractions in the area. It lies northwest of Mevagissey and can be reached from the B3273 St Austell road. Superbly restored Victorian features include lakes and ponds, an Italian Garden, an extensive valley garden with a splendid collection of tree ferns, and huge productive gardens and fruit houses.

MYLOR

Between the city of Truro and seafaring Falmouth is the parish of Mylor, dense with trees and bordered by tidal creeks. A small network of country lanes north of Falmouth links Mylor Bridge, Mylor Churchtown, Restronguet Passage and Mylor Creek. There was once a royal dockyard at Mylor Churchtown where, during the 19th century, the Falmouth packet ships that delivered mail worldwide were repaired and victualled. The Church of St Mylor is in a superb position and has some unique features – a turret rises from its west gable and it has Norman doorways and a fine interior. The gravestones of Mylor are instructive and entertaining. The headstones of Joseph Crapp, near the east window, and of Thomas James, smuggler, near a fork in the churchyard path, bring a smile to your face. Due south from Mylor Bridge, the attractive village of Flushing faces Falmouth just across the river, and a passenger ferry links the two.

NARE HEAD

Nare Head is the focus of a truly beautiful stretch of coast that borders the parishes of Gerrans, Veryan and St Michael Caerhays, between the Roseland Peninsula and Dodman Point. The easiest approach to the area is along the A3078 then on an unclassified road that leads to the village of Veryan, noted for its unique and elegant church and for its remarkable thatched round houses and is definitely worth a visit.

The Church of St Symphorian is impressive, with a dark tower of mottled stone. There are a number of beaches along the shores of Gerrans Bay and Veryan Bay. The best beaches are at Pendower and Carne where there is good parking and access to Nare Head. To the east is the quiet little village of Portloe, which has a small car park at its eastern end. Further east again is a beach at Porthluney below Caerhays Castle, a picturesque, 19th-century replacement for an older building, which has a fine woodland garden.

NARE HEAD

NEWQUAY

NEWQUAY

Newquay is geared unashamedly to its splendid beaches, of course, and in places there seem to be more hotels and guest houses than breathing space. But there is still a strong sense of the 'old' Newquay. Sea-angling trips are available; a good way of appreciating the marine environment and the sea-going traditions of this Cornish town.

The town is lively. The beaches and broad, busy streets with shops, pubs and clubs make Newquay the epitome of bright and breezy holiday-making. Yet there are quiet corners in flower-filled parks and gardens. Attractions include a zoo and fun pools and a swimming pool at the Water World in Trenance Leisure Park off Edgcumbe Avenue.

The Elizabethan manor house of Trerice (National Trust) lies just 3 miles (4.8km) southeast of Newquay. It is an exquisite building. The Elizabethan gardens have long since disappeared but the Trust has laid out the south side of the old garden with fruit trees in a classic 17th-century pattern. There is a restaurant in the Barn and a collection of antique lawnmowers in the hayloft.

PERRANPORTH

The Porth of 'Perran' is the small river channel that slices through the sands into Perran Bay. This is proper golden sand country. A great swathe of it runs north from Perranporth and, at low tide especially, offers the pleasure of beach walking into the distance. But don't walk too far – at the northern end of the beach is a military training area. It is because of the drifting sands here that Perranporth has had three St Piran's churches. The first, dating from the 6th or 7th century, was abandoned as early as the 11th century and, though rediscovered in the 19th century, has been buried again in the sand for its own preservation. The second church was abandoned in the 15th century and the latest was built in a village nearby.

NEWQUAY

Perranporth is a very pleasant resort, which has benefited from being at the heart of 'Poldark Country', a welcome marketing image drawn from the Poldark novels that were later adapted into a popular television series, and illustrate what life was like in Cornwall in the late 19th century. The early books in the saga were written by Winston Graham during the time he lived in Perranporth and many local features inspired the books. He developed his image of the Cornish coastline featured in Poldark from a composite of the coast from Perranporth to Crantock, near Newquay. Perranporth itself was the model for Nampara, the fictional setting of the stories.

PROBUS

The village of Probus boasts the tallest church tower in Cornwall. It is over 123 feet (37.5m) high and is lavishly decorated. The village also boasts one of Cornwall's most interesting gardens. This is Probus Gardens, a demonstration garden of great variety where much good work is carried out and where keen gardeners can pick up a few tips while they enjoy the varied displays of flowers, shrubs, vegetables and fruit. Probus can be reached along the A390 from Truro or St Austell.

A short distance along the A390 from Probus Gardens is Trewithen Garden surrounding the handsome Trewithen House. The house and garden are open to the public.

REDRUTH

Copper and tin mining created Redruth, and then abandoned it. Nevertheless, from the early 18th century until the middle of the 19th, Redruth was the true capital of Cornish mining. Redruth and the mining country that surrounds it, is now recognised for the importance of its unique industrial archaeology, and in 2006 was designated a World Heritage Site.

In the early days, the extraction method was tin-streaming, whereby tinners sifted through river sand and gravel for fragments of ore. The process caused disturbance, which released a red stain into rivers and streams and it was this that gave the town its name, although in odd reversal from what you would expect: red coming from 'rhyd' for ford, and 'ruth', meaning red.

The town contains some fine architecture, including Georgian, Victorian, neo-Gothic and Art Deco buildings. There is a great deal of brickwork and some startling features, such as the Italianate clock tower on the corner of Fore Street and Alma Place. Leading off Fore Street is Cross Street where there is a house with an external staircase, which was once the home of William Murdock, a Scottish engineer and inventor who worked in Redruth during the late 18th century. Among his many achievements, Murdock developed a lighting system using coal gas, and his home in Redruth was the first house in the world to be lit in this way (in 1872).

Visit

THE LOST GARDENS OF HELIGAN

The story of the 'lost' gardens of Heligan is compelling. From 1780 onwards, the Tremaynes developed 57 acres (23ha) of their property at Heligan as a series of splendid gardens. Nature began to get a hold on the gardens during World War I, when the house became a military convalescent home and most of the 22 gardeners enlisted. The house was used again by the American military during World War II and was later converted into flats, and though the Tremaynes still owned the gardens, they remained untouched. In 1990 the estate was inherited by John Willis who, with others, including Tim Smit, the moving force behind the Eden Project, made tentative inroads into the impenetrable jungle and discovered the intact framework of a magnificent garden. By the end of 1995 the restoration was complete.

Visit

CORNISH ENGINE HOUSES

North of Chapel Porth, standing on a lonely stretch of coastline, is the engine house of the Wheal Coates mine. It is one of many such distinctive buildings, which are a feature of the Cornish countryside, and once housed the engine that provided the essential services of winding, pumping and ventilation for the mine. Wheal Coates is an important relic of the county's industrial past, and has been restored by the National Trust, which cares for much of this historic coast. Chapel Porth lies at the heart of old mining country. The coast path to the south leads to Porthtowan.

Activity

ST MAWES FERRIES

There is a regular ferry service between St Mawes and Falmouth, that is worthwhile simply for the pleasure of crossing the Fal Estuary. Another ferry runs the short distance from St Mawes to Place on St Anthony Head and is a delightful way of visiting the area.

ROSELAND PENINSULA

This beautiful peninsula seems quietly detached from mainstream Cornwall. Flanked on its eastern side by a rock-fringed coast curving north into Gerrans Bay, it is bordered on the west by the River Fal, with Mylor and Feock set opposite. The very tip of the Roseland Peninsula is pierced by the twisting Percuil River that cuts deeply inland to create even smaller peninsulas. The area is famous for St Mawes, St Mawes Castle and for the Church of St Just-in-Roseland. A pleasant alternative to the A3078 onto the peninsula, is to take the A39 southwards from Truro, the B3289, past Trelissick Gardens and then cross the Fal by the King Harry Ferry. Another approach is to take the passenger ferry from Falmouth to St Mawes.

St Just-in-Roseland is an exquisite place. The church stands on the banks of a small creek, its mellow stonework embedded in a garden of shrubs and graceful palm and indigenous broad leaved trees.

ST JUST-IN-ROSELAND

On the promontory of land between Carrick Roads and the Percuil River stands St Mawes, deservedly popular and besieged with moored yachts in summer. On Castle Point to the west stands Henry VIII's St Mawes Castle, a quiet triumph of good Tudor design over function and renowned for its symmetry and decoration. The outer arm of the Roseland terminates at St Antony Head (National Trust) where there is a lighthouse and gun battery with an interesting history. On the east coast, further north, is Portscatho, open to the sea and with excellent sandy beaches nearby.

ST AGNES

Mining made St Agnes. Tin, copper ore and lead from nearby mines were exported from here by sea, but it was a difficult coast for seagoing. To either side of Trevaunance Cove below St Agnes the gaunt cliffs made landing by boat treacherous. Trevaunance had a small cramped harbour, where coal and other materials had to be raised by a winch-and-pulley system and the ore tipped down chutes. Since mining ceased in the early years of the last century, the sea has made a resort of this charming north coast village. Trevaunance Cove is quite small but it commands the seaward end of St Agnes. The village is easily accessible from the A30 yet seems pleasantly detached from a busier Cornwall. It is a convoluted village with a one-way system that may confuse you at first. A row of picturesque cottages, called Stippy Stappy, leads down from the upper village to the valley below. There is a fine little local history museum in Penwinnick Road.

To the west, lies St Agnes Beacon, reached by following Beacon Drive to a National Trust parking area on its north side. A good path leads easily to the summit and to spectacular views along the coast. Just to the south of St Agnes is the sandy cove of Chapel Porth, while north of Chapel Porth,

Activity

CLAY COUNTRY CIRCUIT

The vast spoil tips of the St Austell clay country are composed of feldspar and quartz. The raw clay is stripped from the faces of the pits by high pressure hoses creating flooded pits, their translucent green and blue waters adding to the odd surrealism of this 'lunar' landscape. The best way to appreciate the clay country is to drive through it – explore the area north and west of St Austell between the B3279 and the B3274, which takes in Nanpean, Roche, the Roche Rock and China Clay Country Park at Carthew.

ST AUSTELL

Cornwall's famous clay 'Alps' dominate the landscape around St Austell. However, the town's outlook is marred by the industrial sprawl that surrounds it – the price of vigorous industry. Even when it was a mere village St Austell was the centre of good farming country, open-cast tin extraction and stone quarrying. The town is currently undergoing a multi-million pound regeneration programme, scheduled to be completed in 2010, which promises a large new shopping area, cinemas, entertainment, several bars and restaurants.

St Austell still has some fine traditional buildings. Fore Street and the area around Holy Trinity have been conserved and the Town Hall is in bold Renaissance style, a granite palazzo incorporating a splendid market hall with its interior still intact. The Church of The Holy Trinity has sculpted figures set within niches in the tower, which itself is faced with Pentewan stone from the

standing on a lonely stretch of coastline, is the Towanroath engine house (National Trust). Dating from 1872, it housed the massive steam engine that used to pump water from the Wheal Coates mine.

The coast path to the south leads to Porthtowan through a desolate mining landscape that is rich in wild flowers.

coastal quarries to the south. The pearly-grey stone has a warmer tinge when wet.

To the north of St Agnes, is Cornwall's most startling industrial landscape, from which clay has been extracted on a massive scale. The clay was once used for making porcelain but is now used mainly in paper-making. About three million tonnes are produced in the St Austell area annually. Much waste is generated and the great snowy tips have created a strangely compelling landscape that now hosts the Eden Project with its futuristic biomes.

ST COLUMB MAJOR

St Columb Major set on high ground 5 miles (8km) east of Newquay, was once traffic-bound but a bypass has eased the congestion in its narrow streets, which are enclosed between slate-hung houses. There is some very fine architecture, including an Italianate Gothic building of red and yellow bricks that now houses a bank. Opposite is the attractive Red Lion Inn, and much of the main square dates from the Regency period. The Church of St Columba has a procession arch through the base of its impressive tower.

TRELISSICK

Trelissick is a beautiful woodland park, 370 acres (148ha), overlooking the Fal Estuary; the house is not open to the public. The grounds were laid out with carriage drives and were planted with trees during the 1820s to take full advantage of the picturesque views. The parkland is criss-crossed with pathways, which provide some delightful walks.

In the garden's sheltered position many unusual and exotic plants thrive, including subtropical species from South America and Tasmania. But the gardens are particularly noted for their collection of acid-loving camellias, magnolias and hydrangeas, of which there are more than 100 varieties. The large walled garden has fig trees and climbing plants, and there is a shrub garden. Plants are available in the garden shop and there is an art and craft gallery and a restaurant. Theatrical and musical events are often held here.

TRURO

Truro's great cathedral catches the eye from all quarters. It rises from the heart of the city, its honey-coloured stone and lancet windows reflecting the sun, its great Gothic towers piercing the sky. There is no trace of the Norman castle that once stood at Truro, nor of the Dominican friary that stood on the low ground by the river, but the cathedral makes up for their loss.

Truro's fortunes rose and fell over the years, but by the late 18th century it had become the political and cultural centre of Georgian Cornwall. It was during the last years of the 18th century that such famous features as Boscawen Street and Lemon Street were built. Today Boscawen Street is a broad, cobbled space, entered at both

ends from narrow thoroughfares. The granite façade of the City Hall graces Boscawen Street, and Lemon Street survives as one of the finest examples of a late Georgian street in Britain, its houses perfectly aligned to either side of a broad avenue that climbs uphill.

There are hidden glories in Truro amid the modern developments. From the Moorfield car park, a lane leads to Victoria Square, but parallel and to its right is the elegant Georgian crescent of Walsingham Place. Throughout the heart of Truro, the lanes connecting the main streets are lined with attractive shops, cafés and restaurants. From the west end of Boscawen Street, King Street leads up to the pedestrianised area of High Cross in front of the cathedral. The stylish Assembly Rooms, with a façade of Bath stone, stands nearby.

Seen from its forecourt the cathedral seems crowded in by buildings, instead of being the dominating presence that commands the view from outside the city. But the west front and its soaring towers is exhilarating. The foundation stones of the cathedral were laid in 1880 and the western towers were finally dedicated in 1920. Truro's cathedral is thus a Victorian building. It is Early English Gothic in design but with strong French influences that are seen in the great spires. The interior is glorious. It is vaulted throughout and pillars and arches are in elegant proportion, the air light beneath the great roofs. There are beautiful individual features such as the exquisite baptistry. All that remains of the old parish church of St Mary's is incorporated into the south aisle. Those with an eye for ancient stonework may find the outer wall of the old church a reassuring contrast to the smooth planes of the later Victorian cathedral.

Pydar Street runs north from the cathedral as a pleasant pedestrian concourse. A short distance away is the stylish

Activity

WOODLAND WALKS

North of Truro at Idless, is Bishop's Wood, a pleasant Forestry Commission plantation of mainly conifers but with a mix of broadleaved trees such as birch, hazel and willow. The wood can be reached by driving north from Truro on the B3284 to Shortlanesend, from where side roads lead to Idless. The wood is criss-crossed with broad forest tracks and there is a pleasant walk alongside a busy little stream.

Crown Court, and below here are the pleasant Victoria Gardens. Boscawen Park, by the Truro River, is reached along the road to Malpas. The Royal Cornwall Museum in River Street has an excellent collection of minerals and there are exhibitions covering archaeology and mining. The art gallery has works by John Opie, the 18th-century portrait painter, who was born near St Agnes. Truro is an excellent shopping centre.

TOURIST INFORMATION CENTRES

Mevagissey
St Georges Square. Tel: 01726 844857;
www.mevagissey-cornwall.co.uk

Newquay
Municipal Buildings, Marcus Hill.
Tel: 01637 854020;
www.newquay.org.uk

St Austell
Bypass Service Station, Southbourne
Road. Tel: 0870 4450244

Truro
Municipal Buildings, Boscawen Street.
Tel: 01872 274555;
www.truro.gov.uk

PLACES OF INTEREST

Blue Reef Aquarium
Towan Promenade, Newquay.
Tel: 01637 878134;
www.bluereefaquarium.co.uk

Caerhays Castle
Gorran, St Austell.
Tel: 01872 501310; www.caerhays.co.uk

**Charlestown Shipwreck, Rescue and
Heritage Centre**
Charlestown. Tel: 01726 69897;
www.shipwreckcharlestown.com

China Clay Country Park
Wheal Martyn, Carthew,
St Austell. Tel: 01726 850362;
www.wheal-martyn.com

Cornish Engines
Pool, near Redruth.
Tel: 01209 315027

Cornish Cyder Farm
Penhallow.
Tel: 01872 573356;
www.thecornishcyderfarm.co.uk

The Eden Project
Bodelva, St Austell.
Tel: 01726 811911;
www.edenproject.com

Lost Gardens of Heligan
Pentewan, near Mevagissey.
Tel: 01726 845100;
www.heligan.com

Mevagissey Aquarium
South Quay.
Tel: 01726 843305

Polmassick Vineyard
St Ewe, near Mevagissey.
Tel: 01726 842239

Trelissick Garden
Feock, near Truro.
Tel: 01872 862090

FOR CHILDREN

Cornish Birds of Prey Centre
Winnards Perch, St Columb Major.
Tel: 01637 880544;
www.cornishbirdsofprey.co.uk

Dairy Land Farm World
Tresillian Barton, Newquay.
Tel: 01872 510349;
www.dairylandfarmworld.co.uk

Holywell Bay Fun Park
Newquay. Tel: 01637 830531;
www.holywellbay.co.uk

Lappa Valley Steam Railway
St Newlyn East, near Newquay.
Tel: 01872 510317;
www.lappavalley.co.uk

Newquay Zoo
Trenance Leisure Park.
Tel: 01637 873342;
www.newquayzoo.org.uk

St Agnes Leisure Park
St Agnes. Tel: 01872 552793

Screech Owl Sanctuary
Indian Queens. Tel: 01726 860182;
www.screechowlsanctuary.co.uk

World of Model Railways
Mevagissey. Tel: 01726 842457;
www.model-railway.co.uk

SHOPPING

Camborne
Large covered and open-air market at
Pool, Sat and Sun.

Newquay
Covered market daily.

Par
Large covered market at Stadium Park,
Sat and Sun.

St Austell
Open market in town centre, Fri and
Sat.
Shopping precinct, Old Market House.

Truro
Pannier Market, Mon–Sat.
Lemon Street Market, Mon–Sat.

LOCAL SPECIALITIES

Crafts
Cornwall Crafts Association,
Trelissick Gardens, near Truro.
Tel: 01872 864084
Mid Cornwall Galleries,
St Blazey Gate, near St Austell.
Tel: 01726 812131;
www.mid-cornwall-galleries.co.uk

SPORTS & ACTIVITIES
ANGLING
Sea

Mevagissey Shark & Angling Centre.
Tel: 01726 843430
National Boatmen's Association,
Newquay. Tel: 01637 876352

Coarse

Porth Reservoir, near Newquay.
Tel: 01637 877959

BEACHES

*Lifeguards, where indicated, are on
summer service. Dogs are not allowed on
several beaches from Easter Day to 1st
October. During winter, when dogs are
allowed, owners must use poop scoops.*

Chapel Porth

Long stretch of sand, reduced greatly
at high tide. Surfing. Lifeguard.

Crantock Beach

Backed by sand dunes. Estuary
dangerous for swimming. Lifeguard.

Crinnis Beach, Carlyon Bay

Long beach, very popular.

Fistral Beach

Large, popular, international surfing
venue. Lifeguard.

Great Western

Surfing beach. Lifeguard.

Holywell Bay

Large sandy beach with dunes, surfing.
Lifeguard.

Lusty Glaze

Backed by cliffs. Lifeguard.

Newquay Watergate Bay

Large west-facing beach.
Can be breezy. Lifeguard.

Perranporth Village Beach

Popular beach. Lifeguard.

Porth Beach

Safe bathing.

Porthtowan

Large busy beach. Lifeguard.

Portreath

Popular north-facing beach.

Roseland Peninsula

Small beaches in St Mawes and
Portscatho.

St Agnes Trevaunance

Small and popular, but greatly reduced
during highest tides. Surfing.

Tolcarne Beach

Surfing. Lifeguard.

Towan Beach

Large sandy beach. Lifeguard

BOAT TRIPS
Mevagissey and Newquay
Booking offices at harbours.
Truro
River trips from Town Quay or Malpas
to Falmouth. Enterprise Boats.
Tel: 01326 374241/ 313234;
www.enterprise-boats.co.uk

CYCLE HIRE
Newquay
Cycle Revolution, 7 Beach Road.
Tel: 01637 872634
Mevagissey
Pentewan Valley Cycle Hire,
1 West End, Pentewan.
Tel: 01726 844242;
www.pentewanvalleycyclehire.co.uk

**COUNTRY PARKS & NATURE
RESERVES**
Tehidy Country Park
Near Camborne.
Tel: 01209 714494

ANNUAL EVENTS & CUSTOMS
Camborne
Trevithick Day, Apr.
Charlestown
Regatta Week, late Jul.
Mevagissey
Mevagissey Feast Week, Jun.
Newquay
Cornwall Gardens Festival, mid-Mar
to May.
Hot-Air Balloon Festival, May.
British National Surf Championships,
Jul.
RAF St Mawgan International Air Day,
early Aug.
Pro-Am Surf Championships, Aug.
World Life Saving Championships,
Fistral Beach, Aug.
Championship Gig Racing, Sep.
Newquay Music and Flower Festival,
Sep.
St Mawes
Town Regatta, Aug.

TEA ROOMS

Charlotte's Tea House

Coinage Hall, 1 Boscawen Street,
Truro, TR1 2QU
Tel: 01872 263706

This lovingly restored tea house is
on the first floor of the Coinage Hall.
Victorian uniforms, china cups and
antiques add to the charm. The menu
offers sandwiches and delicious
set teas – cream teas with light,
homemade scones and high teas with
sandwiches and irresistable cakes.

The Quarterdeck at the Nare Hotel

Carne Beach, Veryan, TR2 5PF
Tel: 01872 501111
www.narehotel.co.uk

The sea views from the informal
all-day Quarterdeck restaurant are
breathtaking. The set tea menu is
a real treat and best enjoyed on the
terrace in summer. Opt for the classic
cream tea – scones, clotted cream, jam
and sandwiches.

Trenance Cottage Tea Rooms and Gardens

Trenance Lane, Newquay, TR7 2HX
Tel: 01637 872034
www.trenance-cottage.co.uk

Escape the bustling beach in this
award-winning Georgian tea room.
You can lunch on fresh local crab,
home-baked pasties and local cheese
ploughman's, or peruse the extensive
tea list, which offers a brew that
matches your meal or one of the
homemade cakes. Cream teas are also
a speciality.

Carnewas Tea Room and Garden

Bedruthan, St Eval,
Wadebridge, PL27 7UW
Tel: 01637 860701

The dramatic coastline at Bedruthan
Steps is renowned for its spectacular
cliff-top views. Take in the view with
a cream tea or a plate of cakes from
the National Trust tea room on the
cliff-top, which is housed in the office
building of the old Carnewas iron mine.

VERYAN

Roseland Inn

Philleigh, Truro, TR2 5NB
Tel: 01872 580254

A lovely, peaceful setting near the village church, a rose-clad frontage and an unspoilt bar with a homely atmosphere combine with good cooking to make this 17th-century pub a real find. Dine on local farm meats and fish landed at St Mawes in the low-ceilinged bar, with its slate floors, comfortable cushioned settles and winter log fires. The stable door leads to a suntrap terrace.

Pandora Inn

Restronguet Creek, Mylor Bridge, Falmouth, TR11 5ST
Tel: 01326 372678
www.pandorainn.com

Arrive early at this thatched, 13th-century waterside inn, bag a seat on the pontoon and gaze across the creek and its bobbing boats. On inclement days, retreat to the rambling bars and find a cosy corner amongst the nautical memorabilia. There's St Austell ale on tap, good home-cooked food (braised lamb shank, seafood platters, local sea bass) and summer afternoon teas.

Driftwood Spars Hotel

Trevanaunce Cove, St Agnes, TR5 0RT
Tel: 01872 552428
www.driftwoodspars.com

Flowers baskets introduce a dash of colour to this 17th-century whitewashed inn just 110 yards (100m) from one of Cornwall's best beaches and stunning coastal walks.

Lizard Peninsula

CADGWITH

COVERACK

FALMOUTH

GUNWALLOE

HELFORD

HELSTON

KYNANCE COVE

LIZARD DOWNS

LIZARD POINT

MULLION

PORTHLEVEN

INTRODUCTION

The Lizard Peninsula is a large area of downland fringed by sea cliffs of variegated serpentine and slate. The peninsula ends at Lizard Point, the most southerly point in Britain. Along its coastline lovely beaches line the edge of coves and bays. The Lizard is famous for the rare plants that grow on its spacious heathland and on its coastal fringe. To the north of Lizard Point is the Helford River where a softer landscape of wooded creeks and quiet villages leads on to the great natural harbour of Falmouth. At the western gateway to the Lizard is the busy town of Helston.

HOT SPOTS

Unmissable attractions

Admire the multi-coloured serpentine rock, dramatic black cliffs and coves at Kynance Cove and Mullion...visit Helston, a pleasant market town famous for its Flora Day Festival...enjoy walking and cycling around leafy Cadgwith and Coverack...explore the National Maritime Museum Cornwall on Falmouth's waterfront or enjoy Regatta Week in August...look for ancient artefacts on Lizard Downs...go for peaceful walks on the Helford Estuary... take in the views at Lizard Point – Britain's most southerly point.

1

1 Falmouth
Busy with all types of vessels, Falmouth's attractive harbour is backed by whitewashed cottages and lush green countryside.

2 Lizard Point
Visitors to the café at Lizard Point, England's most southerly point, enjoy far-reaching sea views. The area is renowned for its craggy cliff scenery, wooded vales and windswept downs.

3 National Seal Sanctuary
This centre, in the village of Gweek, near Helston, rescues and rehabilitates sick or abandoned seals before releasing them back into the wild.

163

6 Cadgwith
Fishing boats are drawn up on the small beach in the tiny village of Cadgwith, situated on the eastern side of the Lizard Peninsula. Local fishermen fish daily for crab, lobster, shark, mullet and mackerel.

4 Mullion Cove
The small harbour at Mullion is in the care of the National Trust. The boats here land mainly crabs, lobster and crawfish.

5 Helford Estuary
Pretty cottages nestle in the sheltered, tree-lined tidal creeks of the tranquil Helford Estuary.

6

CADGWITH

Thatched and slate-roofed cottages crowd together at Cadgwith between encroaching hillsides and cliffs. A slim shingle beach runs to either side of a rocky promontory called the Todden. Beyond all this, sea and sky are full of light. Cadgwith is best visited on foot; there is a car park on the high ground above the village, from where a path leads down to the village. Fishing boats still work from Cadgwith's beach where pilchards were once landed in vast quantities until the fishery declined in the early 20th century. Today Cadgwith's fishermen use inkwell-shaped pots to catch lobster and crab, and gill nets to catch cod, pollack, monkfish and other species. The old buildings, known as cellers, where the pilchards were salted and pressed for oil, have been converted for modern use.

The small building on the cliff to the north of the cove was a coastguard watch house that was built more than 100 years ago. A short walk along the coast path to the south of Cadgwith (with the sea on your left) leads to the spectacular Devil's Frying-Pan, a huge gulf in the vegetated cliffs where a sea cave collapsed centuries ago leaving an arch of rock connecting both sides.

The Lizard area is especially noted for the variety and value of its plant life. Pink thrift, the powder-blue squill, cliff bluebells and kidney vetch grow in profusion here, but insignificant-looking plants may well be very rare and vulnerable. Visitors are asked not to pick even the most prolific wild flowers and to take care while walking.

COVERACK

Coverack is open to the sea, the village seeming to cling precariously to the edge of its low cliffs and harbour walls. There is a through road, but it is allowed only grudging passage by a steep and awkward corner. Pilchard fishing was the mainstay of Coverack from the medieval period until the early

20th century and the village still has a raw edge of the sea to it. The authentic atmosphere of the old village has survived the impact of more modern development that has attached to it. And if you wonder why a Cornish fishing village should have a Paris Hotel, it is named after a ship that was stranded off the coast of Coverack in 1899.

Just over 2 miles (3.2km) north of Coverack is St Keverne, a village full of character with a compact square and an impressive church. It served the dual purpose of spiritual and navigational guidance, as its ribbed spire was a landmark for local fishermen. This stretch of the coastline was treacherous to larger vessels, especially around the offshore reef known as the Manacles, a vivid name made even more menacing by its derivation from the Cornish *Maen Eglos*, the Church Stones. On the inner walls of St Keverne's beautiful church, and within its churchyard, the many memorials to drowned sailors make poignant reading that is worthy of a Joseph Conrad novel. It is impossible to visit here without considering the high price to human life of great maritime traditions, but there are a number of good pubs in the square to ease any melancholy thoughts with some suitable refreshment.

FALMOUTH

Vessels of all types and sizes still bustle in and out of Falmouth's harbour, lending excitement and atmosphere to one of the world's largest natural harbours. Falmouth developed as a port after Henry VIII built Pendennis and St Mawes castles, the guardians of the Fal Estuary. Both are built in the distinctive clover-leaf design and St Mawes is particularly renowned as a fine example of military architecture. Visitors here can explore the dungeons, barrack rooms and cannon-lined castle walls.

During the late 17th century the port became a packet station, from where small, fast-sailing brigantines took mail to northwest Spain, and in later years to North America, the West Indies and South America. Gold and silver bullion was carried and the packets provided a passenger service. By the 1830s over 40 packets worked out of Falmouth. They were well-armed against privateers, French naval hostility and even Algerian pirates. The crews supplemented their meagre wages with smuggling and by carrying unofficial goods; there are rich tales of villainy and swashbuckling. The packet service had transferred to Southampton by 1850 but Falmouth's position as a major port was secured by a vigorous pilchard fishery, the development of Falmouth docks and a thriving shipbuilding industry. Ship repair, bunkering, cargo handling and yacht building are local industries that continue today.

Falmouth's rather straggling form gives it less unity than might be expected of a port, as the town follows the riverside through a chain of linking main streets, but this makes it intriguing to explore. It is centred on The Moor, once just a muddy creek and now emphatically urban, and it is here that you will find the Falmouth Art Gallery, well worth a visit, on the upper floor of the old Passmore Edwards Free Library. As well as changing exhibitions there are permanent displays of paintings

Activity

FALMOUTH AFLOAT

Various river and sea cruises are available from Falmouth's Prince of Wales Pier and from other boarding points around the estuary. Ferries leave for Flushing and St Mawes, and when the tide allows, there are cruises upriver to Malpas from where a five-minute bus ride connects with Truro. An enjoyable trip can be made upriver to Tolverne on the Roseland Peninsula. If you are confident of having good sea legs, there are trips along the coast and then up the Helford River; evening cruises on the Fal are another option along with sea-angling trips from the Prince of Wales Pier.

COVERACK

LIZARD PENINSULA

Activity

LIZARD LAKES

Cornwall has few natural lakes of any size but there are reservoirs that make a pleasant change from the sea. The Argal Waterpark is only about 2 miles (3km) from Falmouth along the A394. The reservoir here is tree-fringed and very peaceful, with much birdlife and pleasant paths skirting the shoreline. Coarse fishing is available all year. The fly-fishing season is from March to October. Stithians Lake is within easy reach of Falmouth and Helston along the A394. There is a car park on the east side of the lake near the dam and another at its north end, near the watersports centre.

including those of Henry Scott Tuke, the Victorian painter who spent his last years near Falmouth. From The Moor, Webber Street leads to the Prince of Wales Pier. Market Street is the first of Falmouth's long chain of streets that leads along the riverfront. The walk along Market Street, Church Street and Arwenack Street should be varied by diversions to the town quays from where there are superb panoramic views across the river mouth.

Some of Falmouth's many engaging features include the 111-step Jacob's Ladder that leads up from The Moor, and watch out for the recurring theme of Falmouth's 'Opes', the passageways, which run between the town's buildings.

Pendennis Castle is located on the headland to the east of Falmouth and is easily reached from the waterfront. Of the several very pleasant beaches along Falmouth's southern seafront, Gyllyngvase is the largest and most popular. The National Maritime Museum Cornwall, on Falmouth's waterfront, includes the National Small Boat Collection of 120 boats. Various craft are also moored alongside the museum's pontoon from where they are regularly sailed. Cornwall's maritime heritage is portrayed through reconstructions,

FALMOUTH

GUNWALLOE

GUNWALLOE

special exhibitions, audio-visual and interactive displays, including hands-on operation of model boats, and there are live demonstrations of boat construction. There is also a unique tidal gallery with windows that reveal the rise and fall of the tide, and breathtaking views across Falmouth Harbour from a 95-foot (29m) tower.

Use the Park & Float and sail to the museum in a classic ferry.

GUNWALLOE

The road to Gunwalloe ends at Church Cove where an intriguing little 15th-century church nestles close to the edge of eroded cliffs. The cliffs have been stabilised by huge rocks to create a breakwater. North of the church is the noisily named Jangye-ryn Cove. Inland lie extensive sand dunes; a golf course crowns the green swell of the higher land in rather odd counterpoint.

The coastline is often lively, as it is west facing and open to boisterous seas. Shipwrecks were common during the days of sail when vessels became trapped within the horns of Mount's Bay; the price of not giving the Lizard a wide enough berth was grief on Gunwalloe's shoreline. The name of Dollar Cove below the church reflects the loss of a Spanish treasure ship in the 1780s.

Halzephron Cove and Gunwalloe Fishing Cove lie just to the north of Church Cove and can be reached along the coast path. The National Trust has solved the problem of scattered parking at Gunwalloe with a screened car park on the approach to Church Cove. Though the problem of sea erosion is another matter. The sea is threatening to break through the neck of land between Dollar Cove and Church Cove and large blocks of granite have been tipped onto the beach to break the force of the waves.

HELFORD

There is irresistible romance attached to Helford and its tree-shrouded river and creeks. The

177

price is that the area can become uncomfortably busy during popular holiday periods. Lovely though the village is, the dense nature of this serene landscape rewards those who explore further than Helford itself. The countryside is passive, compared with the extremes of the coast, and though access along the river bank is limited in places, there are a number of fine walks to be enjoyed from Helford.

Just to the west lies gorgeous Frenchman's Creek, romanticised by both Sir Arthur Quiller-Couch and Daphne du Maurier and still enchanting today, even when the falling tide reveals an expanse of mud. A good path leads east from Helford to the coast at Dennis Head and to St Anthony and Gillan. These quiet and peaceful places are best visited on foot; parking is difficult and is not encouraged.

A seasonal passenger ferry from Helford sails to Helford Passage on the north bank, from where the National Trust's Glendurgan Garden and the adjacent Trebah Garden can be visited. Glendurgan is one of the great subtropical gardens of the southwest, situated on the banks of the Helford River near Mawnan Smith. Acid-loving hydrangeas, camellias and rhododendrons flourish amidst lovely woodland and there is an engaging maze. Trebah Garden has a fine water garden among its attractions. The smaller garden at Penjerrick, just over a mile (1.6km) north of Mawnan Smith, is where Chilean firebushes, magnolias and azaleas flourish.

HELSTON

Helston is the true gateway to the Lizard Peninsula. It was a port until the silting of the River Cober landlocked the town, but historically its main importance was as the trading centre of the area and as a Coinage town. It thrived throughout the medieval period and for several centuries thereafter despite fluctuations in the metal mining industry. The name of Coinagehall

FRENCHMAN'S CREEK

Street is witness to the town's history and its generous width reflects its history; the town is still a very good shopping centre. There is a grand view down Coinagehall Street to the Gothic-style gateway of the bowling green and to the fields beyond. The Guildhall dominates the top of the street and the nearby Victorian Market House is quite stylish for its time.

There is an interesting museum in the Market House. Church Street runs down to the left of the Market House and then up to the Church of St Michael, which is 18th century and rather dull. Church Street and the adjoining Cross Street have good Georgian façades and the area has a strong period atmosphere. Helston is famous for its annual Furry, or Flora Dance. Proximity to the Penrose estate (National Trust walks) and Loe Bar adds to Helston's many attractions. Penrose can be reached from the Coronation Gardens and Boating Lake at the bottom end of the town.

Off the B3293 St Keverne road, located about 3.5 miles (5.6km) from Helston, is Trelowarren House. It has been the home of the Vyvyan family since the early 15th century and has craft workshops and an art gallery.

KYNANCE COVE

Victorian 'excursionists' first visited Kynance with their painting kits and sketch books and the cove was visited by a poet, Tennyson, and a prince, Albert. Kynance satisfied perfectly the romantic ideal of the picturesque in Nature. The whole of the beach is awash at high tide and emerges fresh and shining as each day dawns. The gnarled monoliths of serpentine rock that rise at intervals from the beach create a beautiful seascape. The largest is Asparagus Island, with Steeple Rock and the Sugar Loaf lying between it and the mainland. Part of the charm of Kynance lies in its unexpectedness, hidden as it is below the edge of the sometimes unnerving flatness of the Lizard Peninsula.

181

LIZARD PENINSULA

The cove and the cliff land to the east are in the care of the National Trust, which has provided a car park above Kynance and a viewpoint for visitors with disabilities. Descent to the cove is steep, and the return is quite strenuous. Great care should be taken if swimming off the cove – the tide comes in rapidly and the currents close to shore are dangerous to the unwary.

The Kynance area is of great biological importance. Rare species grow here including sedges and tiny liverworts. Spiders, moths and even a rare European woodlouse are also found here. The mild climate and a maritime environment partly explain the richness of local wildlife.

LIZARD DOWNS

The Lizard Downs are rich in ancient artefacts that date from a time when early man found reasonable grazing on the poorly drained soil. The serpentine soil also supports a remarkable variety of rare plants. The Lizard's mild climate encourages these plants but the main reason for the area's unique botanical nature is that the Lizard was joined to the European land mass thousands of years ago, when these plants spread and flourished on what are now the peninsula's coastal fringes.

There are subtle distinctions between species and a specialist's knowledge is required to identify many of the plants. But everyone can recognise and enjoy the attractive Cornish Heath, Erica Vagans, a type of heather found in substantial quantities only on The Lizard. It has dark green leaves and spikes of small pink or lilac flowers. Closer to the cliff-tops, the blue spring squill, the pink thrift and the creamy sea campion contribute to a mosaic of wild flowers in spring and summer.

LIZARD POINT

Lizard village is a convenient base to explore Lizard Point and its coastline. You can park at the Point, where there is an old lifeboat station

LIZARD POINT

MULLION

that has long been superseded by the modern station at Kilcobben Cove to the northeast. The view seaward is exhilarating and the air can be mild even in midwinter, but when the tide is out, swathes of pungent smelling seaweed may dull the edge of the bracing sea air. Choughs returned to breed in Cornwall on Lizard Point in 2001 after an absence of 50 years and the RSPB operates a Chough Watchpoint during spring.

The coast path leads west above high cliffs. To the east it passes through a green, sheltered landscape above cliffs draped with the invasive Hottentot Fig, or mesembryanthemum. The Lizard's position, jutting out into the Channel approaches, has made it dangerous to vessels. For a mile (1.6km) seaward off Lizard Point the sea tumbles in frightening overfalls during stormy weather. To the northeast lies the blunt promontory of Black Head and beyond here the deadly Manacles Reef.

The fortress-like Lizard Lighthouse dominates the coast to the east. A warning light was first lit here in 1612. Today's light flashes every three seconds and can be seen in clear weather from up to 29 miles (46.7km) away. The fog signal is delivered by siren every 60 seconds.

About 1.5 miles (2.4km) east of Lizard Point is Church Cove, and its attractive little church of Landewednack. The cove is reached on foot from the car park past thatched cottages. A short walk south along the coast path leads to the remarkable cliffside site of the Lizard-Cadgwith lifeboat house.

MULLION

Mullion is a large village a short distance inland from the harbour at Mullion Cove. There is a nice sense of anticipation on first approaching Mullion and the village lives up to expectations – a bustling place with an excellent variety of shops, art and craft galleries and good pubs. The Church of St Melanus has a

189

remarkable collection of bench-ends depicting characters, including a jester and a monk. Mullion Cove is fascinating. Big cliffs and sea stacks, gold-leafed with yellow lichen, enclose the narrow inlet and its substantial piers. Offshore lies the bulky mass of Mullion Island, flickering with seabirds.

The coast to the south is pleasantly remote, especially around Predannack Head and Vellan Head, with delightful coast walks to either side of the cove. Just to the north of Mullion is Polurrian Cove where there is a large sandy beach and further north again is the popular Poldhu Cove with its sandy dunes.

PORTHLEVEN

Porthleven was noted for its shipbuilding and fishing industries. Remarkably, both have survived and the village remains a truly Cornish place. The centrepiece inner harbour is lined along its quays with an interesting mix of galleries, shops, pubs, restaurants and cafés. On the north side of the outer harbour is a wave-cut platform of deeply pocketed and riven slate where a huge boulder, the Giant's Rock, is exposed at low tide. It is believed to be a glacial 'erratic' carried here embedded probably in an ice floe during the last Ice Age.

Victorian villas on the South Quay create a pleasing background to the harbour road and bustling quayside. To the southeast, a road lined with cottages leads along the cliff edge and Loe Bar Road, leads to a car park, for the short walk to Loe Bar and the Penrose estate.

Porthleven harbour was always vulnerable to westerly storms and even today the breakwater and outer harbour do not hold off the sea entirely. There is more than one famous news picture of storm waves crashing over the entrance to Porthleven harbour. Sea conditions can be deceptive and if the sea is rough and the tide high you should never walk out along the outer piers. Swimming in this area is dangerous.

PLEASE CALL AT THE BACK DOOR
MARY AND THE... CORNER.
MORE ITEMS IN BACK GARDEN

FERNLEIGH COTTAGE

OLD IRON
WHEEL
£25

ST KEVERNE

TOURIST INFORMATION CENTRES
Falmouth
11 Market Strand, Prince of Wales Pier.
Tel: 01326 312300
Helston
79 Meneage Street.
Tel: 01326 565431

PLACES OF INTEREST
Falmouth Art Gallery
Municipal Buildings, The Moor.
Tel: 01326 313863;
www.falmouthartgallery.com
GARDENS
In addition to the larger gardens
listed in this section, there are a
number of smaller gardens open to
the public, notably Carwinion at
Mawnan Smith, Potager Garden at
Constantine, and Bonython Manor
near Cury Cross Lanes.
Tel: 01872 322900;
www.gardensofcornwall.com
Glendurgan Garden
Mawnan Smith, near Falmouth.
Tel: 01326 250906

Godolphin House
Godolphin Cross, Breage.
Tel: 01736 763194;
www.godolphinhouse.com
**Goonhilly Satellite Earth Station
Experience**
Near Helston.
Tel: 0800 679593;
www.goohilly.bt.co.uk
Helston Folk Museum
Old Butter Market, Church Street.
Tel: 01326 564027
National Maritime Museum Cornwall
Discovery Quay, Falmouth.
Tel: 01326 313388;
www.nmmc.co.uk
National Seal Sanctuary
Gweek. Tel: 01326 221361;
www.sealsanctuary.co.uk
Pendennis Castle
Falmouth.
Tel: 01326 316594
Penjerrick Garden
Budock, Falmouth.
Tel: 01872 870105;
www.penjerrickgarden.co.uk

Poldark Mine and Heritage Complex
Wendron, near Helston.
Tel: 01326 573173;
www.poldark-mine.co.uk

Trebah Gardens
Mawnan Smith, near Falmouth.
Tel: 01326 250448;
www.trebah-garden.co.uk

Trelowarren
Mawgan, Helston.
Tel: 01326 221224;
www.trelowarren.com

Trevarno Estate
Crowntown, Helston.
Tel: 01326 574274;
www.trevarno.co.uk

FOR CHILDREN
The Flambards Experience
Helston.
Tel: 0845 601 8684
(24-hour information line);
www.flambards.co.uk

SHOPPING
Falmouth
High Street, Market Street and Church
Street.

Helston
Market Coinagehall Street,
Mon and Sat.

LOCAL SPECIALITIES
CRAFTS
Beside The Wave
10 Arwenack Street, Falmouth.
Tel: 01326 211132;
www.beside-the-wave.co.uk

Nic Harrison Ceramics
73 Meneage Street, Helston.
Tel: 01326 560521;
www.nicharrison.com

Trelowarren Gallery
Helston.
Tel: 01326 221567.

PERFORMING ARTS
Falmouth Arts Centre
Church Street, Falmouth.
Tel: 01326 314566;
www.falmoutharts.org

Princess Pavilion
Melvill Road, Falmouth.
Tel: 01326 211222

SPORTS & ACTIVITIES
ANGLING
Sea
Falmouth, Mullion, Cadgwith.
Coarse
Argal Reservoir, Penryn, Falmouth.
Tel: 01837 871565
Stithians Lake, Redruth.
Tel: 01209 860301
BEACHES
Lifeguards, where indicated, are on summer service. Dogs are not allowed on several beaches from Easter Day to 1st October. During winter, when dogs are allowed, owners must use poop scoops.
Falmouth
Swanpool: sandy with facilities nearby; Gyllngvase: large, popular, family beach, safe bathing.
Gunwalloe
Lifeguard.
Kennack Sands
Large sandy beach, with numerous rock pools.
Kynance Cove
Steep beach at low tide. Steep steps to the beach.

Maenporth
Sheltered with level access.
Poldhu Cove
Near Mullion. Popular beach with dunes. Lifeguard.
Praa Sands
Huge beach popular with families and surfers. Lifeguard.
BOAT TRIPS
Falmouth
Prince of Wales Pier.
Regular passenger ferries to St Mawes and Flushing. River cruises to Roseland Peninsula and Truro.
Sea cruises.
www.enterprise-boats.co.uk
BOWLING
Falmouth Bowling Club, Penryn.
Please contact the Tourist Information Centre.
CYCLING
A network of quiet lanes offers good cycling between the main roads and main centres. Cycling is not permitted on public footpaths or on the coast path.
www.cyclecornwall.com

CYCLE HIRE
Mullion
Atlantic Forge. Tel: 01326 240294

GOLF COURSES
Falmouth
Falmouth Golf Club, Swanpool Road.
Tel: 01326 311262;
www.falmouthgolfclub.com
Helston
Helston Golf and Leisure.
Tel: 01326 565103
Mawnan Smith
Budock Vean Golf and Country Club.
Tel: 01326 252100;
www.budockvean.co.uk
Mullion
Mullion Golf Club, Cury.
Tel: 01326 240685;
www.mulliongolfclub.co.uk

HORSE-RIDING
St Keverne
Creek Pony Riding Holidays,
Treglossick. Tel: 01326 280297

SAILING
Mylor
Mylor Sailing School, Mylor Harbour.
Tel: 01326 377633;
www.mylorsailingschool.co.uk

WATERSPORTS
Coverack
Coverack Windsurfing Centre.
Tel: 01326 280939;
www.coverack.co.uk
Stithians Lake
Between Falmouth and Helston off
the A394.
Tel: 01209 860301;
www.swlakestrust.co.uk

ANNUAL EVENTS & CUSTOMS
Gig racing is a major sport in Cornwall.
Races are held in the summer at such
venues as Cadgwith and Porthleven.
Falmouth
Falmouth Regatta Week, Aug. Maritime
events including racing of Falmouth
classic yachts as well as dinghies.
www.falmouthweek.co.uk
Helston
Helston Flora Day, 8 May, or previous
Sat if 8 May is a Sun or Mon. The
famous Furry Dance is performed
throughout the day starting at 7am.
Market stalls.

TEA ROOMS

Sarah's Crab Shop
Cadgwith Cove, Helston, TR12 7JX
Tel: 01326 290539
Sarah is dedicated to fresh crab and you'll find her tiny shop-cum-café smack beside the beach and the boats that supply her with the crab that she sells from the shop window. Buy it by the pound or have it made into a memorable crab sandwich. She will also prepare you a delicious cream tea – savour both at tables by the beach.

Polpeor Café
Lizard Point, The Lizard, TR12 7HJ
Tel: 01326 290939
At Britain's most southerly café, perched high on the cliffs on Lizard Point, you can watch waves crashing onto rocks and choughs wheeling around the cliffs while you tuck into a local crab salad and sandwiches or a traditional cream tea. On fine summer days, the suntrap terrace right on the cliff edge is the place to eat.

Roskilly's Croust House
Tregellast Barton Farm, St Keverne, Helston, TR12 8NX
Tel: 01326 280479
www.roskillys.co.uk
Roskilly's is a family-run, working organic farm where they make one of Cornwall's much-loved ice creams, as well as clotted cream, fudge, preserves, jams and juices. A great family day out on the farm can culminate with a home-made lunch, tea and cake, or a delicious cream tea with warm scones and their famous clotted cream and fruity jams. All can be washed down with apple juice or cider made on the farm.

Shipwrights Arms

Helford, Helston, TR12 6JX
Tel: 01326 231235

Stunningly located on the banks of the Helford Estuary, the narrow approach road is restricted to pedestrians only. This is a pretty thatched pub with a terraced garden and picnic benches on the water's edge. The bar is traditional, with rustic furnishings and plenty of nautical bits and pieces. Summer buffet lunches and evening barbecues draw the crowds.

Cadgwith Cove Inn

Cadgwith, Ruan Minor,
Helston, TR12 7JX
Tel: 01326 290513
www.cadgwithcoveinn.com

An unspoilt hamlet of thatched cottages is the setting for this old-fashioned, bustling local. Crab sandwiches and a pint of Sharp's Doom Bar provide the perfect lunch, best enjoyed on the sunny terrace with views across the cove.

Halzephron Inn

Gunwalloe, Helston, TR12 7QB
Tel: 01326 240406

The 500-year-old Halzephron Inn commands an enviable position perched high above Gunwalloe Cove. There's a warm welcome inside the two low-ceilinged bars and bistro-style restaurant. Expect to find local ales on handpump and menus that utilise the best local ingredients. Arrive early for tasty seafood chowder, cod in beer batter, and chargrilled beef with Madeira sauce.

The Ship

Porthleven, Helston, TR13 9JS
Tel: 01326 564204

This old fisherman's pub enjoys a magnificent position looking across the harbour. The view is best appreciated from the terraced lawns behind the pub. On winter days, climb the flight of steps and take in the view from the warmth of a window seat in the bar. Here, quaff tip-top Sharp's beers and refuel on pub food, perhaps monkfish in bacon or chargrilled lamb steak.

Land's End

Cornwall's 'First and Last' peninsula is a vivid landscape of spectacular cliffs and golden beaches that are washed by the clear Atlantic waters. Inland, small fields and narrow, twisting lanes lie embedded within a network of granite hedges that are smothered with wild flowers. Prehistoric monuments stand amidst the heather and pale grass of the moorland hills and the rugged north coast is noted for the industrial archaeology of its abandoned tin mines. Here you'll discover the ideal conditions for sailing, surfing and rock-climbing or painting, birdwatching and sea-fishing.

LAND'S END

Unmissable attractions

Enjoy Lands End Peninsula – a world of spectacular promontories, such as Gurnard's Head and Logan Rock...explore prehistoric stone circles and burial chambers on Penwith Moors...discover the north coast and St Ives, the archetypal Cornish fishing village, where fishing and tourism happily co-exist...walk the dramatic coastal path at Zennor...get lost in the quaintness of Mousehouse...paddle at Porthcurno's superb beaches or enjoy a truly memorable evening watching a perfomance at the Minack Theatre...take a boat from Penzance to the golden Isles of Scilly and visit the exotic gardens at Tresco Abbey House.

1

1 Zennor

The dramatic coastal path near Zennor follows a succession of rugged points and headlands above high weathered granite cliffs. Below, are hidden sandy coves and clear blue sea.

2 Porthcurno Beach

Porthcurno completes the idyll with its glorious golden beach. Famed for its granite cliffs and sea of Mediterranean blue. Porthcurno Valley is also known for its historic telecommunications links. Visit the Telegraph Museum located just above Porthcurno car park.

3 Rock climbing, Zennor
Cornwall's challenging granite sea cliffs around Zennor are popular with rock climbers.

4 Tate St Ives
Overlooking Porthmeor Beach, Tate St Ives exhibits the very best of Cornish contemporary art. Many of the works of art on display depict the extraordinary light that is found in and around St Ives.

5

5 Mousehole

On the western edge of Mount's Bay, Mousehole's quaint houses and cottages, linked by narrow alleyways and passages, crouch above the high-walled little harbour that once sheltered a prosperous pilchard-fishing fleet.

HAYLE

Hayle's industrial past was sustained by Victorian tin and copper mining, a fact reflected in local names as Copperhouse and Foundry. Unfortunately, it is Hayle's rather straggling extent and its general decline that have denied it picturesque appeal; but awareness of the town's industrial past makes a visit rewarding for those looking for the history under the skin. A brisk walk along the eastern side of the harbour and along the northern side of the large tidal pond, Copperhouse Pool, though not entirely scenic, is worthwhile. The contrast between the dereliction of Hayle's harbour area and the spaciousness and brightness of its nearby beaches is quite startling. Access to several miles of golden beach, popular with families, sunbathers and surfers, can be gained from Hayle by following the road through the village of Phillack and out to a car park amid shoals of chalets. The town has a good choice of

Activity

BIRDS OF A FEATHER

Hayle Estuary is an important winter feeding ground for wild birds, a bonus to birdwatchers in spring and autumn especially. Some very rare sightings are possible during autumn migrations when vagrant species from America may be pushed off their north-to-south migratory path and driven across the Atlantic to Cornwall. The best site is at Lelant Saltings to the west of Hayle. Access is from just off the A30 on the Penzance and St Ives road by the Old Quay House Inn.

shops, galleries and craft shops, restaurants and several pleasantly down-to-earth pubs.

LAMORNA

Lamorna is the most sheltered of the narrow valleys that lead gently down to the south-facing shores of Mount's Bay. The road that leads down to Lamorna Valley is narrow and can become congested during

Bank Holidays. It is a delightful road nonetheless, descending through shady woodland to reach an unexpected bay that is fringed by granite cliffs. This is Lamorna's theme; there is charm around every corner if you are just willing to explore. Granite from Lamorna's hillside quarries were used to build many Victorian lighthouses and such famous features as the Thames Embankment. On the way down to the cove is the Wink Inn, a classic Cornish pub with an engaging atmosphere. The 'wink' signifies the blind eye that the gentry and local vicars often turned to old-time smuggling. Lamorna's rugged granite quay is a pleasant place to linger on a warm day.

A mile (1.6km) west of Lamorna Valley in a field alongside the B3315 is a stone circle dating from the early Bronze Age – the famous Rosemodress, or Boleigh Circle of 19 upright stones. It is popularly known as the Merry Maidens, from entertaining but ridiculous legends of young girls turned to stone for dancing on a Sunday. In nearby fields are two tall standing stones, the Pipers, who suffered the same fate. They are all more likely to have been ceremonial sites of the Bronze-Age peoples. A short distance west of the Merry Maidens, and close to the road, is the Tregiffian entrance grave. Also from the Bronze Age, it comprises a kerbed cairn with a chamber roofed with slabs.

LAND'S END

The symbolic geography of Land's End demands a visit although the natural attractions of the area are perhaps best enjoyed outside the busiest holiday periods. Do not expect to find yourselves romantically alone during daylight hours – except in a Force 9 gale.

But while rugged weather may enhance the Land's End experience for the true romantic, the venue's numerous covered attractions are enjoyable as wet-weather alternatives. They include interesting

HAYLE

exhibitions, gift shops, craft centres and galleries, and the 'Last Labyrinth' electronic theatre where the real experiences of the Cornish coast are cleverly, if sometimes ironically, simulated. There is a good choice of eating places within the complex and the Land's End Hotel is in a splendid position overlooking the Longships Lighthouse. There may be queues on the approach on popular Bank Holidays and during peak holiday periods.

Open access on foot, of course, is time-honoured and for those who prefer a more robust approach than by car, the coast path can be followed to Land's End from Sennen in the north (1 mile/1.6km) or from Porthgwarra in the southeast (3 miles/4.8km).

MARAZION

Marazion is a town first and foremost. You may earn yourself a deservedly frosty glance if you call this ancient borough anything less. It was the main trading port

Activity

END-TO-ENDERS

The long walk from John O'Groats, at the northern tip of Scotland, to Land's End has attracted a multitude of people eager to cover the 603 miles (970km) in one piece. Famous End-to-Enders include Ian Botham and Jimmy Saville. Some began anonymously and then became famous, like the round-the-world walker Ffyona Campbell. Most make the trip for personal reasons, or for charities, which have benefited hugely from such efforts. There is even an official End-to-Enders Club. Straightforward walking remains the obvious challenge, but there have been numerous variations from four wheels to two wheels, bed-pushes, to nude cyclists (but only for the last few sunny Cornish miles). A few determined souls have done it via the coast . Saltings to the west of Hayle. Access is from just off the A30 on the Penzance and St Ives road by the Old Quay House Inn.

Insight

DISHY FISH

Pilchards are not so easy to come by these days, but a good Cornish fish merchant will have a splendid selection of fish to tempt you. Mackerel are a good fleshy fish, though oily; the old Cornish treatment was to 'souse' them in vinegar and bay leaves, but today smoked and peppered mackerel are available. And very tasty too. Hake, cod, haddock and ling are all meaty, flavoursome fish. Best of all are John Dory and turbot. Expensive Dover and lemon sole will tempt the taste, but test the treasury. Monkfish is good for imaginative cooking. Bon appetit!

shops to browse and pleasant pubs, restaurants and cafés.

Marazion Beach offers safe bathing and is a glorious suntrap. It offers good windsurfing especially during spring and autumn, when conditions are breezy. The quiet village of Perranuthnoe, just a short distance southeast with a south-facing beach also provides reasonable surfing at times. A few miles further east lies Prussia Cove, a secluded rocky inlet of great charm reached most rewardingly by a pleasant 2-mile (3.2km) walk along the coast path.

The great complement to Marazion is the castellated Isle of St Michael's Mount (cared for by the National Trust), the most romantic offshore island in Britain and a matching image to Mont St Michel off the Normandy coast. The Mount was dedicated to St Michael after claims of miraculous sightings of the saint by 5th-century fishermen. Even today shafts of celestial light seem drawn to St Michael's Mount

of Mount's Bay until an upstart Penzance developed its own markets and port during the 16th century. But Marazion has remained as distinctive as its lovely name, which derives, rather plainly, from the Cornish word for market. There is an informative little museum at the town hall in Market Square, antique and craft

ST MICHAEL'S MOUNT

although a view of angels is perhaps less likely. In its day the Mount has been monastery, prison, and castle-under-siege. The Mount is nicely defined as a part-time island by successive high tides during which it may be reached by a pleasant boat trip. At low tide the approach is on foot along a fine cobbled causeway.

MOUSEHOLE

Quaintness clings to Mousehole's name like a cat. But 'Mouz'l', as it should be pronounced, is a fishing village of strong character, though the days are long gone when its harbour was crammed with pilchard-fishing boats. The name derives from obscure roots. Its old Cornish name is *Porth Enys*, meaning 'the landing place by the island'. The small island offshore from Mousehole is called St Clement's after a hermit who is said to have maintained a warning light.

Tempting alleyways and passages wriggle between sturdy cottages in Mousehole and the harbourside Ship Inn rounds things off with a flourish. The far end of Mousehole's tiny harbour has a splendid inner wall of irregular granite blocks, a perfect subject for imaginative photography or sketching. There are some shops, including craft shops, cafés and restaurants. Mousehole was not built for motor vehicles and is best explored on foot. There is a car park by the harbour but it fills quickly during busy periods. The other is to park just outside the village on the road from Newlyn.

A steep hill leads inland from Mousehole to the village of Paul where the Church of St Pol de Leon has some impressive features. These include a memorial to the Mousehole crew of the local lifeboat, the Solomon Browne. They died heroically near Lamorna during an appalling storm in December 1981 after repeated attempts to save the eight people aboard the wrecked cargo vessel Union Star. The road out of Mousehole to the west leads up the dauntingly steep Raginnis Hill. Partway up is the famous Mousehole Bird Hospital, a refuge for countless injured birds many of which are the victims of oil pollution. The recovery cages often contain several very vocal birds.

PENDEEN

Pendeen is made up of a straggling line of small communities that were once linked to tin and copper mines on the north coast of the Land's End peninsula. The smaller villages of Carnyorth, Trewellard, Boscaswell and Bojewyan make up the roll call of this last of Cornwall's coastal mining communities. The area's appeal is based on the startling conjunction of a fractured mining landscape and the raw beauty of the Atlantic coast. Pendeen's Geevor Mine was the mainstay of the larger area but the mine closed in 1991 in the face of international market pressures, and in spite of a spirited campaign by local people to save the industry. Surface freehold of Geevor is owned by Cornwall County Council and the complex has been imaginatively developed as a heritage centre, with mine workings, a museum and a fascinating underground tour.

Just south of Geevor is the National Trust's Levant Engine House, which is reached from Trewellard. At Levant, the silken power of steam is harnessed to a restored working beam engine.

PENWITH MOORS

Penwith Moors run parallel to the north coast of the Land's End Peninsula through an undulating series of hills that are crowned with granite tors.

The high ground begins at Rosewall Hill just west of St Ives and is continuous throughout the beautiful parishes of Zennor and Morvah. Smaller areas of moorland continue the westward-leading sequence to Chapel Carn Brea above the wide, flat coastal plateau of Land's End itself. The moorland

PENDEEN

PREHISTORIC PEDAL

A cycle ride to ancient monuments – 20 miles (32km), mostly moderate with some steep gradients. From Penzance, take the A30 west to Drift; turn right and pass Drift Reservoir then keep ahead following signs for 'Brane' and 'Carn Euny'. Visit Carn Euny Iron Age village on foot, then retrace your route and follow signs to Sancreed. Turn left beyond Sancreed church; continue to St Just then follow the B3306 north to Pendeen. Beyond Pendeen, go left, signed 'Pendeen Lighthouse'. After half a mile (800m) go right to Pendeen Manor Farm and, with permission, view the Iron Age underground chamber. Return to the B3306 and continue left to Morvah. Turn right beyond Morvah, signed 'Madron' with a steep climb and descent to Bosullow. Opposite Men-an-Tol Studio, a track leads to Men-an-Tol, a probable remnant of a prehistoric burial chamber. From Bosullow follow the road to reach Lanyon Quoit. Return to Penzance through Madron.

is a splendid counterpoint to the peninsula's outstanding coastline and is easily accessible from a number of points. Penwith Moors are noted for their ecological value and for their unique concentration of Neolithic, Bronze Age and Iron Age remains that include burial chambers, settlements, stone circles and standing stones. Most of the northern moors are at the heart of the Environmentally Sensitive Area within which farmers are compensated for working in sympathy with the traditional structure of the ancient landscape.

PENZANCE

Penzance has a sunny, friendly character gained from its south-facing position on the most sheltered part of Mount's Bay and from the bustle of its many attractive streets. It has the only promenade in Cornwall and it is a lengthy one, with wonderful views. The open-air, Art Deco Jubilee Swimming Pool rounds off the harbour end of the

promenade. Penzance harbour is small but has a busy atmosphere and a mix of vessels from fishing boats to visiting yachts; the passenger boat to the Isles of Scilly leaves from the outer pier.

A pleasant approach to the harbour, from the busy Market Place, is down the diverting Chapel Street where there are antique and craft shops, pubs and eating houses. Penzance's attractive main street, Market Jew Street, is enhanced further by a raised granite terrace. There are shops of all kinds here, and in the pedestrianised Causewayhead that leads inland from Market Place. Towards the sea, and to either side of the Morrab Road, are Morrab Gardens and Penlee Park; the former is a lovely ornamental garden, the latter houses the Penlee House Gallery and Museum. The gallery stages excellent temporary exhibitions, often of work by the 19th- and early 20th-century Newlyn-based painters, such as Stanhope and

Elizabeth Forbes, Walter Langley and 'Lamorna' Birch, who lived in the area from 1880 to 1940. The museum has good displays of local archaeology and the environment.

To the west, Penzance merges with Newlyn, the major fishing port in the southwest. Newlyn harbour is full of life and colour. Scores of fishing boats of all types and sizes work from here in spite of the increasing difficulties of the modern international industry. The large fish market bustles with activity in the early morning as boats land a remarkable variety of fish. Parking at Newlyn is difficult, and most visitors find that a walk along Penzance's spacious promenade and on along the seafront to Newlyn is a pleasant alternative, which can be combined with a visit to the Newlyn Art Gallery along the way.

Just outside Penzance is the National Trust's Trengwainton Garden, a complex of five walled gardens set amid mature woodland. It is at its best during the spring and early summer, with an exquisite display of magnolias, acacias, camellias, azaleas and rhododendrons. It can be reached via Heamoor, or from Tremethick Cross on the St Just road.

Penzance has a summer festival called Golowan that lasts for ten days in mid-June and involves numerous cultural events and entertainment. It culminates in Mazey Day when the streets of Penzance are closed to traffic and the main street, Market Jew Street, hosts a busy street fair.

PORTHCURNO

The golden sand of Porthcurno's beaches and the clarity of its sea supports Cornwall's claim to be an alternative to the Mediterranean. Under a blazing summer sun, the comparison is apt. Granite towers and pinnacles lie embedded in the steep vegetated slopes that encircle the bay and the superb sand lies deeply against the shoreline. Some of the adjoining beaches are covered

Visit

HIGH PLACES

Northeast of Sennen, the ground rises to Chapel Carn Brea, a smooth-browed hill (National Trust) and reached by turning off the A30 Land's End road at Crows-an-wra. There is a car park by the roadside from which a path leads to the summit. At various times in the past, Chapel Carn Brea was the site of a Bronze Age burial chamber, a medieval chapel and a beacon.

at high tide but the main Porthcurno beach is always available, clean, sparkling and luxurious.

For many years Porthcurno was the centre of international cable telegraphy. From here, undersea telegraph cables communicated with the rest of the world and, at one time, the Cable and Wireless Company ran a training college in the Porthcurno Valley. In 1994, Porthcurno beach and its adjacent cliff land was given to the National Trust by the company, which had

229

relocated its main training facilities to Coventry. There is a fascinating telegraph museum housed in underground chambers within the old Porthcurno college complex just inland from the large car park.

The visitor to Porthcurno is really spoiled for choice. The main beach is marvellously persuasive for wriggling the toes; but to either side lie lovely coastal walks. Eastward is the famous Logan Rock, a vast monolith that once rocked at the touch of a finger but is less responsive now, and westward is Minack Theatre – a sun-drenched site that seems to grow out of the natural rock– Porth Chapel beach and the little Church of St Levan. St Levan can also be reached along the narrow road that climbs steeply uphill from Porthcurno. There is a car park by the church. All around Porthcurno Bay you will find sheltered coves, such as Penberth, and exquisite tidal beaches, and the eastern side is flanked by the superb headland of Treryn Dinas.

PORTHGWARRA

Porthgwarra lies to the southwest of Porthcurno and is sheltered from the prevailing Atlantic winds by high ground that culminates at the magnificent granite cliff of Chair Ladder at Gwennap Head, the most southerly extent of the Land's End Peninsula. At Porthgwarra, tunnels have been carved through the softer rock of flanking promontories to allow access to the beach by donkey and trap in the days when neighbouring farmers collected seaweed to fertilise their fields. The cliff-top walks to the west are magnificent and the area is noted for rare species of birds that often make landfall here during spring and autumn migrations.

ST IVES

St Ives' rare character springs from its fishing traditions, its artistic inheritance, and its tourism industry. There is a clash of style amongst all three at times, but St Ives has survived such competing interests.

231

Visit

TRENCROM HILL

The fine rocky hill of Trencrom, the site of an Iron-Age encampment, stands above the Hayle Estuary and can be reached from Lelant or from the B3311 St Ives to Penzance road. Trencrom is in the care of the National Trust and there is a small car park on its southern side. The path to the summit is short and steep in places, but the views are outstanding. Just west of Trencrom is the little village of Nancledra from where the green and peaceful Towednack Valley runs north to the sea through a gap in the coastal hills.

Not only is the town the archetypal Cornish fishing port, it also has magnificent beaches of silken sand that offer safe family bathing and surf to sing about. The town greatly benefited greatly from the opening of the Tate St Ives in 1993.

The gallery stands above Porthmeor Beach, its curves and crests are as white as the waves below. The paintings on display are by leading artists of the St Ives School including Patrick Heron, Peter Lanyon and Terry Frost. It is a joy to find such paintings within the very landscape that inspired them. The view seaward from the gallery's roof terrace is worth crossing the world for. Before the Tate opened, the Barbara Hepworth Museum and Sculpture Garden was the most important artistic attraction here and still remains very popular.

But St Ives is a delight overall because of its narrow, canyon-like streets, ubiquitous granite cobbles, and clear, sea-mirrored light. The parish church of St Ia is one of the finest in Cornwall. St Ives harbour area, known locally as 'Downlong', is a maze of exquisite vernacular granite buildings where you catch satisfying glimpses of shady courtyards and passageways.

And there are always those superb beaches to escape to for a paddle or a walk: Porthminster to the south is sheltered and calm;

ST IVES

ST IVES

Porthmeor to the north is more lively and popular with the surfing crowd.

There are several smaller beaches at the harbour and in the lee of the Island, the breezy, green promontory that juts out to sea from a low-lying neck of land. The price of all this is potential overcrowding at the busiest holiday periods. Avoid dawdling through St Ives by car and be prepared for close-quarters humanity in the narrow Fore Street and along the busy harbour front. There is a park-and-ride scheme at Trenwith above the town and another at Lelant Station, southeast of the town, which uses a little branch line. Artistic ambience – and, at times, pretension – means that St Ives has numerous galleries and craft shops. There is an excellent town museum at Wheal Dream, and many pubs and restaurants of quality and character.

ST JUST

At the heart of this sturdy Cornish town, you will find a generous market square. At the eastern corner of the crowded square stands the parish church, a lovely 15th-century building in good weathered granite, with a square tower and a handsome interior. Market Square has a number of friendly pubs and there are cafés and a good selection of shops in which to browse within the square and in the streets that radiate from it. St Just is the ideal base from which to explore the famous mining coast of the Land's End Peninsula.

The elegant headland of Cape Cornwall lies to the west; it is rugged, yet shapely and its rounded summit is crowned with the chimney stack of a long defunct mine. On the southern edge of the cape is Priest's Cove from where small fishing boats work. From the cove, a stony track leads up to the rocky headland of Carn Gloose from where the impressive burial chamber of Ballowall lies about 150 yards (137m) inland. The cape, and coastline to either side, is in the care of the National Trust.

To the north lies Kenidjack and the Nancherrow Valley, a historic mining area being preserved by the National Trust. A mile (1.6km) north of the town along the B3306 is the village of Botallack and the coastal area is rich in old mine buildings.

SENNEN

The Atlantic truly begins at Sennen's Whitesand Bay where the west-facing beaches can be exhilarating when the surf is high. Gwenver Beach to the north is a 'serious' surfing and body-boarding beach that is also good for sunbathing, though close attention should be paid to safety flags and to lifeguards. Tidal currents can be fierce. Sennen Beach is the larger of the two. It is less adventurous but just as delightful and is easily accessible from the car park at Sennen Cove.

Sennen is in two halves. The village is on the higher ground alongside the A30. Sennen Cove has the main attractions of the beaches and fine granite cliffs to the south. A

Activity

A SCENIC ROUTE

One of the finest scenic drives in England is to the north of Sennen along the B3306 coast road. The section between Morvah and St Ives is quite spectacular. The road winds its sinuous way between mottled moorland and the patchworked web of Iron Age fields that cluster together along the narrow coastal plateau above a glittering sea. There are pubs along the way and several cream-tea havens.

car park at the far end gives access to the cliff path and to Land's End on foot. This southern end of the cove spills into the ocean and has a brisk sea-going atmosphere with a narrow quay edging into the sea – to be avoided during rough conditions – and a lifeboat house with a modern lifeboat. The nearby wood and granite Round House contained the capstan that was used for hauling boats out of the water. It is now a craft shop and gallery.

ZENNOR

ZENNOR

Storm-tumbled cliffs and wheeling gulls, guard Penwith's wild, Atlantic shoreline. The sleepy village of Zennor with its rough tawny hills slope down towards the echoing sea cliffs. Between hills and sea lies a narrow coastal plateau of small irregular fields whose Cornish 'hedges' of rough granite date from the Iron Age. Because of its antiquity this long-farmed landscape has earned Zennor protected status for ecological and archaeological reasons. Such vulnerability should be taken into account when visiting Zennor and its surrounding countryside. Below the car park is the Wayside Museum; it is crammed with exhibits about farming, mining, archaeology and folklore. Zennor's Church of St Senara lords it rather handsomely over the village.

Zennor has an endearing myth of a mermaid. The mermaid was said to have seduced a local chorister into the dark waters below the lofty Zennor Head. On quiet evenings, the smooth heads of seals perpetuate the legend and an attractive bench-end motif in the church encourages the tale.

Access to Zennor Head and to the coast path is on foot down a narrow lane that starts behind the Tinner's Arms. Zennor Head has a flat top, but its western flank is spectacular. Towering cliffs fall darkly into a narrow gulf, the sea crashes white against the shoreline far below. If you can tear yourself away from thoughts of mermaids, it is an invigorating 6-mile (9.6km) walk eastwards to St Ives along some of the most remote coastline in Cornwall.

THE ISLES OF SCILLY

Famously known as the 'Fortunate' or the 'Sunshine Islands', the beauty and uniqueness of the Isles of Scilly don't require exaggeration.

The hundred or so islands and islets that make up the archipelago lie 28 miles (45km) west-southwest of Land's End as the crow flies. Only

Activity

LIVE AND LIVELY ENTERTAINMENT

There are numerous slide shows and talks in the local community hall of each of the islands. Island boatmen especially are noted for their salty wit. Cricket is popular, and visitors are often press-ganged into making up teams. Watch out, extremely competent islanders are often matched against mainland elevens. Don't even think of mentioning mid-on or mid-off.

BEST BOAT TRIPS IN BRITAIN?

Scillonians are outstanding seamen, and the tradition of small-boat handling is maintained by the fishermen and boatmen who run pleasure trips. These trips are an essential part of getting the best from a visit to the Scilly Isles. The inter-island launches connect daily to St Mary's and also make trips between the islands. Some of the best trips are to the outlying unin-habited islands, where seals, puffins and seabirds can be seen at close quarters.

five islands are inhabited – St Agnes, Bryher, St Mary's, St Martin's, and Tresco – and together they offer a rare combination of seascapes, golden beaches and crystal-clear sea, with quiet green corners inland.

Bryher lies in the northwestern group of islands that include Tresco. It is 1.5 miles (2.4km) long and barely half a mile (800m) across at its widest point. Bryher faces Tresco across the narrow channel of New Grimsby Sound and island life is focused on the beaches that fringe the Sound. Here boats draw up at a granite quay, or at the jetty, built as one of Anneka Rice's famous television 'challenges' to extend landing times on Bryher and now known as 'Annequay'.

At just over 1 mile (1.6km) wide, St Agnes has a serene atmosphere. It is the most southerly of the group and is separated from St Mary's by the deep water channel of St Mary's Sound. The Turk's Head Inn and the Post Office are at the hub of the community. To the east the main island is linked by a narrow sandbar to the smaller tidal 'island' of Gugh and off its western shore is the protected bird island of Annet. Beyond Annet lie the dramatic Western Rocks – reefs that end at the Bishop Rock Lighthouse.

The most northerly island in the group, St Martin's is 2 miles (3.2km) in length and just over half a mile (800m) wide. Landing on St Martin's can be adventurous at certain states of the tide, when walking the plank to reach the sandy shore from launches is necessary. Walking here is exhilarating, though the lure of fine beaches such as Great Bay on the northern shore tends to distract.

St Mary's is the largest of the Isles of Scilly. Its main settlement of Hugh Town is the marine metropolis of the islands, and it is from Hugh Town Quay that the passenger launches leave for the exciting sea-trips that are an essential part of holidaying on Scilly. There are beaches on the north and south side of Hugh Town, the southern bay of Porth Cressa being particularly delightful. A footpath follows the coastline for a 9-mile (14.4km) circuit, passing several well-preserved prehistoric sites on the way. Early flower growing developed in Scilly from the late 1860s. Daffodils and narcissi are still exported from the islands, but the trade has declined in recent years.

Tresco has a helipad and lies at the sheltered heart of the islands. It is a private domain where there is an atmosphere of carefully regulated life and of gentle pace. The exquisite subtropical gardens surrounding Tresco Abbey House are the main focus here. A priory to St Nicholas was established by Benedictine monks during the 12th century; the scant ruins which remain are now incorporated into the Abbey Gardens, where gigantic ice plants, Mimosa, Aloes, Burmese Honeysuckle, Australian Scarlet Bottle-brush, Dracaenas and other superb exotics line the terraced pathways. Dogs must be kept on leads on Tresco.

TOURIST INFORMATION CENTRES

St Ives
The Guildhall, Street-an-Pol.
Tel: 01736 796297.

Penzance
Station Road. Tel: 01736 362207.

Hayle
Putting Green, Lethlean Lane
(seasonal opening). Tel: 01736 754399.

St Just
Library, Market Street
(seasonal opening). Tel: 01736 788669.

Isles of Scilly
Hugh Town, St Mary's.
Tel: 01720 422536;
www.simplyscilly.co.uk

PLACES OF INTEREST

Abbey Garden and Valhalla
Tresco, Isles of Scilly.
Tel: 01720 424105; www.tresco.co.uk

Barbara Hepworth Museum and Sculpture Garden
Barnoon Hill, St Ives.
Tel: 01736 796226; www.tate.org.uk

Chysauster Ancient Village
Newmill. Tel: 07831 757934;
www.english-heritage.org.uk

Geevor Tin Mine
Pendeen.
Tel: 01736 788662; www.geevor.com

Levant Mine & Beam Engine
Trewellard. Tel: 01736 786156

Marazion Town Museum
Town Hall, The Square.

Minack Theatre and Exhibition Centre
Porthcurno.
Tel: 01736 810181; www.minack.com

Mousehole Wild Bird Hospital & Sanctuary
Raginnis Hill. Tel: 01736 731386;
www.mouseholebirdhospital.org.uk

Newlyn Art Gallery
New Road, Newlyn. Tel: 01736 363715;
www.newlynartgallery.co.uk

Penlee House Gallery and Museum
Penlee Park, Morrab Road.
Tel: 01736 363625.

Penwith Gallery
Back Road West, St Ives.
Tel: 01736 795579.

Porthcurno Telegraph Museum
Tel: 01736 810966;
www.porthcurno.org.uk

St Ives Museum
Wheal Dream. Tel: 01736 796005.

Isles of Scilly Museum
Church Street, Hugh Town.
Tel: 01720 422337; www.iosmuseum.org

St Michael's Mount
Marazion. Tel: 01736 710265;
www.stmichaelsmount.co.uk

Tate St Ives
Porthmeor, St Ives.
Tel: 01736 796226; www.tate.org.uk.

Trengwainton Garden
Madron. Tel: 01736 363148.

Trereife
Trereife, Penzance. Tel: 01736 362750;
www.trereifepark.co.uk.

Trewidden Garden
Buryas Bridge, Penzance.
Tel: 01736 366800.

FOR CHILDREN
Paradise Park
Trelissick Road, Hayle.
Tel: 01736 751020;
www.paradisepark.org.uk.

SHOPPING
Penzance
Chapel Street has a good selection of antiques and crafts shops.

St Ives
Galleries and crafts shops, Fore Street.

LOCAL SPECIALITIES
Crafts
Gem and Jewellery Workshop,
Pendeen. Tel: 01736 788217.
Chapel Street, Penzance.
The Round House, Sennen.
Tel: 01736 871859;
www.round-house.co.uk

PERFORMING ARTS
Acorn Theatre
Parade Street, Penzance.
Tel: 01736 365520.

Minack Theatre
Porthcurno.
Open-air performances in summer.
Tel: 01736 810181; www.minack.com

SPORTS & ACTIVITIES
ANGLING
Sea
St Ives, Penzance, Mousehole

Coarse
South West Lakes Trust.
Tel: 01566 771930.

243

BEACHES

Lifeguards, where indicated, are on summer service. Dogs are not allowed on several beaches from Easter Day to 1st October. During winter, when dogs are allowed, owners must use poop scoops.

Carbis Bay

Safe bathing. Lifeguard.

Hayle

Hayle Towans; Mexico Towans, Upton Towans and Gwithian: Generally safe bathing. Surfing. Lifeguards.

Marazion

Windsurfing. Lifeguard.

Penzance

Long Rock Beach: shingle and sand, safe bathing.

Perranuthnoe

Safe bathing, but sandbank may form at centre of beach.

Porthcurno

Safe bathing, but take care during high tide. Lifeguard.

Sennen

Gwenver: Bathing between flags only; Sennen: Blue Flag Award, Seaside Award. Surfing, bathing between flags only. Lifeguard.

St Ives

Porthminster: safe bathing. Lifeguard. Porthmeor: Blue Flag Award, Seaside Award, surfing beach, generally safe bathing. Lifeguard.

BOAT TRIPS

Penzance

Isles of Scilly Steamship Company. Day trips to Isles of Scilly.
Tel: 0845 710 5555;
www.ios-travel.co.uk

Marine Discovery

Excursions to see seals, seabirds, sharks and dolphins.
Tel: 01736 874907;
www.marinediscovery.co.uk

St Ives

Sea cruises from the harbour.

CYCLE HIRE

Hayle
Hayle Cycles, 36 Penpol Terrace.
Tel: 01736 753825

Penzance
The Cycle Centre, New Street.
Tel: 01736 351671
Pedals Bike Hire, Kiosk 17, Wharfside
Shopping Centre.
Tel: 01730 360600

HORSE-RIDING

Lelant Downs
Old Mill Stables.
Tel: 01736 753045

Penzance
Mulfra Trekking Centre, Newmill.
Tel: 01736 361601

WATERSPORTS

Hayle
Shore Surf School.
Tel: 01736 755556;
www.shoresurf.com

St Ives
WindandSea, 25 Fore Street.
Tel: 01736 794830

ANNUAL CUSTOMS & EVENTS

Hayle
Hayle Heritage Week, Jul–Aug.

Isles of Scilly
Tresco Marathon, Apr
Camel Rock Festival, Aug
Gig racing throughout the summer
from St Mary's Quay.
World Gig Racing Championships, early
May.

Mousehole
Sea, Salts & Sail Festival, Jul

Newlyn
Newlyn Fish Festival,
Aug Bank Holiday Mon.

Penzance
Golowan Festival and Mazey Day, Jun.
www.golowan.co.uk

St Ives
St Ives Feast Day, early Feb.
St Ives Festival of Music and the Arts,
early Sep.

St Just
Lafrowda Day – Community Festival,
Jul.

TEA ROOMS

Orangery Café
Penlee House Gallery & Museum,
Morrab Road, Penzance, TR18 4HE
Tel: 01736 363625
www.penleehouse.org.uk
Follow an enlightening gallery tour
with lunch or afternoon tea in the café.
Cakes and pastries are freshly baked,
lunches include crab sandwiches,
quiche, and fish pie.

Godrevy Café
Godrevy Towans, Gwithian,
Hayle, TR27 5ED
Tel: 01736 757999
Godrevy Café stands isolated within the
dunes at Godrevy Beach. Beautifully
designed, it has spacious terraces
which make the most of the view, and
an unusual attic dining space. It's open
all day, so come for breakfast, coffee
and cakes, a light lunch, or watch the
sunset as you dine from the evening
restaurant menu.

Porthgwidden Café
Porthgwidden Beach,
St Ives, TR26 1PL
Tel: 01736 796791
www.porthminstercafe.co.uk
A relaxed and intimate café with a
notably Moroccan feel on the quietest
beach in St Ives. Call in for smoked
salmon and scrambled egg, freshly
baked muffins or croissants from 8am.
Pick a sunny day and head straight
for the terrace for cracking views.
Lunches take in mussels with coconut
and basil broth, and fresh crab
sandwiches. Afternoon teas on the
terrace are an experience to savour as
are the Mediterranean-style dinners in
the evening.

PORTH MOINA

Star Inn
Fore Street, St Just, TR19 7LL
Tel: 01736 788767

St Just's oldest pub has a low-beamed bar, a polished slate floor, glowing coal fires and walls packed with mining and seafaring memorabilia. Pop in to experience the homely, unspoilt atmosphere, the St Austell beer, and a yarn with the locals.

Tinners Arms
Zennor, St Ives, TR26 3BY
Tel: 01736 796927
www.tinnersarms.com

A former tin miners' local, it is now an oasis for walkers tackling the St Ives to Zennor coastal walk. Two open fires warm the bar, filled with flagstones, and pine tables, where you can rest and refuel on Sharp's ales, fresh fish and locally reared meats.

The Gurnard's Head
Treen, Zennor, TR26 3DE
Tel: 01736 796928
www.gurnardshead.co.uk

The imposing Gurn a menu which changes daily and includes fresh Newlyn fish and local farm meats. Crab and fish stew, herb-crusted John Dory and rib-eye steak with red onion marmalade will not disappoint, nor will the Skinner's ales.

Old Coastguard Inn
The Parade, Mousehole, TR19 6PR
Tel: 01736 731222
www.oldcoastguardhotel.co.uk

This one-time coastguard station is perched high above village. Although more of a hotel than pub, there is a light and airy bar with real ale on tap. Contemporary menus take in delicious lunchtime soups, sandwiches and salads, and fresh fish.

USEFUL INFORMATION

OTHER INFORMATION
Coastguard
Dial 999 and ask for the Coastguard Service, which co-ordinates rescue services.

Cornwall Wildlife Trust
Five Acres, Allet, Truro.
Tel: 01872 273939;
www.cornwallwildlifetrust.org.uk

English Heritage
Canada House, 3 Chepstow Street, Manchester.
Tel: 0161 242 1400;
www.english-heritage.org.uk

National Trust in Cornwall
Lanhydrock, Bodmin.
Tel: 01208 74281;
www.nationaltrust.org.uk

Health
Information on health problems is available from NHS Direct.
Tel: 0845 4647
www.nhsdirect.nhs.uk
Dental Helpline
Tel: 0845 063 1188

Environment Agency
Manley House, Kestrel Way, Exeter.
Tel: 08708 506 506

Angling
Numerous opportunities for fishing on farms, lakes and rivers. Permits and licences are available from local tackle shops and TICs.

Public Transport
Timetable for bus, coach, rail, ferry and air services in Cornwall is available from Passenger Transport Unit, County Hall, Truro.
Tel: 01872 322000

Parking
Information on parking permits and car parks in the area is available from local TICs.

Places of Interest

We give details of just some of the facilities within the area covered by this guide. Further information can be obtained from local TICs or the web.

Weather Call

Southwest weather details.
Tel: 09068 500 404

Beaches

Lifeguards, where indicated, are on summer service. Dogs are not allowed on several popular beaches from Easter to 1st October. During winter, when dogs are allowed, owners are asked to use poop scoops. For more information on beaches in Cornwall visit www.cornwall-beaches.co.uk; www.cornwallbeachguide.co.uk

Surf Call

Tel: 09068 360 360

Cycling

A network of quiet lanes offers good cycling between the main roads and centres of the area. Please note that cycling is not allowed on public footpaths or on the coast path. Some woodland areas have excellent cycle routes; leaflets are available from South East Cornwall Discovery Centre.
Tel: 01503 262777;
www.cyclingcornwall.com

INDEX

255

ACKNOWLEDGEMENTS

The Automobile Association wishes to thank the following photographers, companies and picture libraries for their assistance in the preparation of this book.

Abbreviations for the picture credits are as follows – (t) top; (b) bottom; (c) centre; (l) left; (r) right; (AA) AA World Travel Library.

2/3 AA/J Wood; 6 AA/C Jones; 9 AA/J Wyand; 12/13 AA/A Lawson; 14 AA/C Jones; 15t AA/R Moss; 15b AA/N Ray; 16 AA/J Wood; 17 AA/J Wood; 19 AA/R Tenison; 20 AA/C Jones; 23 AA/C Jones; 24 AA/C Jones; 26 AA/R Moss; 28/29 AA/C Jones; 30 AA/J Wood; 31t AA/R Moss; 31b AA/R Moss; 32 AA/A Lawson; 33 AA/J Wood; 35 AA/A Lawson; 38/39 AA/J Wood; 40 AA/J Wood; 43 AA/C Jones; 46 AA/N Ray; 50 AA/C Jones; 53 AA/J Wood; 59 AA/R Moss; 60 AA/R Tenison; 62 AA/J Wood; 64/65 AA/J Wood; 66 AA/J Wood; 67 AA/J Wood; 68t AA/R Moss; 68b AA/J Wood; 69 AA/J Wood; 70 AA/R Moss; 74/75 AA/J Wood; 76 AA/J Wood; 79 AA/J Wood; 80 AA/J Wood; 82/83 AA/J Wood; 85 AA/C Jones; 86 AA/R Moss; 89 AA/C Jones; 90/91 AA/R Moss; 93 AA/J Wood; 94/95 AA/J Wood; 96 AA/R Tenison; 99 AA/J Wood; 100 AA/J Wood; 107 AA/R Tenison; 108 AA/J Wood; 110 AA/J Wood; 112/113 AA/C Jones; 114 AA/R Moss; 115 AA/J Miller ; 116t AA/R Tenison; 116b AA/C Jones; 117 AA/R Tenison; 118 AA/C Jones; 121 AA/R Moss; 122/123 AA/J Wood; 125 AA/R Moss; 126/127 AA/J Wood; 131 AA/J Wood; 132 AA/J Wood; 134/135 AA/J Wood; 138/139 AA/J Wood; 141 AA/J Wood; 142 AA/R Moss; 145 AA/R Moss; 146 AA/J Wood; 155 AA/J Wood; 156 AA/R Moss; 158 AA/R Moss; 160/161 AA/R Moss; 162 AA/C Jones; 163t AA/J Wood; 163b AA/R Moss; 164t AA/J Wood; 164b AA/J Wood; 165 AA/J Wood; 166 AA/J Wood; 170/171 AA/J Wood; 173 AA/C Jones; 174/175 AA/J Wood; 176 AA/J Wood; 178 AA/C Jones; 180 AA/J Wood; 182/183 AA/J Wood; 185 AA/C Jones; 186/187 AA/C Jones; 188 AA/J Wood; 190/191 AA/J Wood; 193 AA/J Wood; 199 AA/C Jones; 200 AA/J Wood; 202 AA/C Jones; 204/205 AA/R Moss; 206 AA/J Wood; 207 AA/J Wood; 208l AA/J Wood; 208r AA/J Wood; 209 AA/C Jones; 210 AA/R Moss; 213 AA/J Wood; 214 AA/R Tenison; 217 AA/C Jones; 218 AA/C Jones; 221 AA/C Jones; 222/223 AA/J Wood; 225 AA/J Wood; 226/227 AA/J Wood; 230 AA/R Moss; 233 AA/C Jones; 234/235 AA/C Jones; 238 AA/J Wood; 247 AA/J Wood; 248 AA/J Wood

Every effort has been made to trace the copyright holders, and we apologise in advance for any accidental errors. We would be happy to apply the corrections in the following edition of this publication.

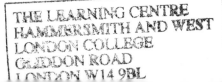